SURVIVAL OF THE SMALLEST
The story of how speech began.

By Wendy Turner

 **New Generation Publishing**

For all the children whose spoken language development is slow and difficult, and for my grandchildren, Samuel and Rebecca, who have reminded me what magic and delight there is when all goes well.

Acknowledgements

Throughout my work on this project I have been constantly touched by the kindness of everyone who has responded to my requests for help. Both in the early days and later, Speech and Language Therapist friends and colleagues have been foremost amongst them.

As time has gone by I have approached specialist authorities in the field of Language Evolution, and their willingness to give advice and encouragement has been truly amazing. I am immensely indebted to all of them for their interest, and can only apologise for the inadequacies of the finished work; those are mine alone.

Last but not least, I want to say how grateful I am to Richard, my husband, for his support and endless patience over many years.

CONTENTS

SURVIVAL OF THE SMALLEST:

the story of how speech began.

PROLOGUE

This is my story. It begins in a tree.

I've climbed as high as I dare, and through the branches I can see my grandmother sitting on the ground below me. She has brought knitting to do while I play, and sometimes when she leans against the bark her cardigan catches on it, because the tree is a pine. Its trunk is rough and resinous, oozing sticky fluid which is difficult to remove from hands and clothes. The scent of pines is good for you, she says.

"Ooh, listen to the wind in the pines!" she will say as we climb the hill to get to the woods. We pause to listen. "Take big breaths!" she says.

Half way up, if I'm thirsty, there's an ice-cold spring, and I can drink from a metal cup attached to the rock by a chain. My grandmother also knows where wild pears grow if we get hungry.

The tree I'm in is familiar. The ends of its lowermost branches have broken off, and their stumps extend at convenient distances up the trunk, so it's easy to haul myself aloft. I sit surrounded by the pine scent, and my mind makes links, storing it as a reminder of the tree, the place and the person. Every sense is alert, taking it all in.

Looking through the pattern of the needles, my view reaches into a hazy distance, to fields and houses, and beyond them to the Longbridge motor factory where my grandfather works.

"Listen for the buzzer!" calls my grandmother. When we hear its long blast I have to climb down and we leave, because he comes home at midday for dinner.

The morning has been filled with a wealth of sensory experiences, ensuring that everything I've seen, touched, tasted, smelt, heard and even felt within my limbs as I moved has added to my bank of knowledge about the place I'm in and the things I can do. My understanding that certain stimuli can have special significance is expanding rapidly, thanks to an older member of my family.

It's strange to think that the processes of finding out about the world were probably much the same for me – a small child in nineteen-forties Britain - as they would have been for our infant pre-human ancestors hundreds of thousands of years ago. They too would have been learning where to find water, fruit in its season, and to recognize certain scents carried on the breeze; they would have felt the cautionary tug of fear regulating the impulse to over-stretch their strength and agility. A sudden particular sound demanding interpretation would have made them sensitive to the responses of older kin. But there was one significant difference between their experiences and mine: I and my family understand and use spoken language.

This complex skill is something we almost take for granted, yet how did it arise? What prompted its beginnings in our early ancestors? And how did its multitude of features accumulate?

And why should I want to write a book about it?

For more than twenty years I worked as a speech and language therapist, mainly helping small children develop various aspects of their communication skills. Usually there was no underlying disorder (such as hearing loss or physical problem) and although their speech and language development was delayed, the stages the children subsequently went through were like those of any child. It was exciting to be involved in approaches and activities which prompted improvement, and to be able to track a fascinating process of growth.

Sometimes the families who came to the clinic were struggling to cope with children who neither understood what was said nor uttered much more than grunts. However, by focusing attention *away* from the act of speaking – by building on whatever associated abilities the children themselves already had, however tentative or rudimentary – it was possible for them to make progress. For families who had been trying to 'make' children talk or correct their mistakes, the experience had been frustrating and distressing, and it was a relief all round when it became clear that you could nurture instead the skills which naturally precede and give rise to spoken language.

As time went by, it occurred to me that ancestral species may well have had abilities which underlie and precede the skills we associate with spoken language. Also, there would be many situations in pre-human history which offered parallels to those we know prompt key features to emerge, and they would certainly have engaged in activities that, in us, are known to foster its growth.

So when I later began reading books about human evolution, I became more and more intrigued by the thought that insights gained through my work with children might throw up some different ideas and perspectives on how those ancient ancestral species might have been communicating and how – somehow – that led to the spoken language of *Homo sapiens*, my family and me.

However, to find the earliest signs of abilities, situations and activities with potential, I soon discovered we'd have to go back in time a very long way indeed.

Before about 6 million years ago, our most ancient primate ancestors lived in trees - African trees – but then the forests began opening out and by 4 million years ago these creatures had embarked on a slow descent.[1] Although for a long while they continued to return to them to sleep or when danger threatened, finally there was no going back. Through all the years that followed, generation after generation of individuals were surviving the heat and the cold, the wet and the dry, and finding their place within a variety of landscapes. Time after time they were faced with changing conditions and different habitats. Everything about them that had previously fitted them for a life in the trees - physically, socially and cognitively - had the potential to be modified and to evolve, if it would keep them alive in these new situations. Their communication system would have been no exception.

Clearly, at a moment somewhere down those years, members that preceded, or were linked to our particular ancestral line, began to transform the way they were using their version of the typical primate system[2] – one that had served them perfectly well thus far. Then, out of a repertoire of vocal calls, signs and signals, they began to construct something much more complex. Their system eventually became an intellectual tool of amazing power, so what was it that prompted them – little by little - to keep on changing what they did?

The usual reasons that have been put forward for why spoken language was needed by ancestral humans are easy to summarize - it was helpful in hunting, in the organisation of a community, and in the selection of mates. It enabled more information to be passed on, especially to the young and it was another form of social 'bonding', influencing relationships. The assumption is clear: the skill arose in response to the needs of adults – they were the ones who 'invented' it. Yet the way we've actually evolved suggests something very different.

Look who's talking
Today, spoken language only arises during infancy. As adults, we certainly need it – our way of life depends on it – but as adults, we cannot develop it.

There is in fact a special window of opportunity for acquiring language skills – and that window is only wide open for the very young.[3] It is then that the process can seem effortless and development is rapid. Even before children are born it is setting seed, and by the time they are four years old, competent, linguistic (or grammatical) communication is normally well established. It's as though in those first critical months and years there's an aspect of the brain's functions which is poised to coordinate the features on which linguistic communication depends. Why should this be? Why does it happen that even in their first year babies are showing an understanding of what's said to them, and will coo and babble, then vocalize, blending sounds together to communicate orally?

What this suggests is that spoken language grows out of the particular conditions, situations and demands typical of infancy, rather than of adulthood.[4] Babies arrive in the world with their systems receptive to whatever stimuli they encounter – and it is the learning style of an immature brain that determines what kind of responses occur. The mature brain can react to demands on the basis of experience and learning, as well as instinct, but the infant brain serves different, immediate priorities. Clearly, the development of spoken language is one of them, otherwise the urgency with which it develops and becomes established is inexplicable if the skill is merely biding its time for later.

Of course, children's earliest efforts may seem far removed from 'proper' speech, but like any emerging physical or mental capacity, the various components of spoken language will develop and establish through being used, and will persist - just because they're available and prove their worth. Naturally, too, the skill is bound to serve its user best, through time, if it can alter its form and its functions to match the changing needs of the growing person. So its scope is slow to stabilize; there's an on-going acquisition of vocabulary as well as a wide range of long and complex utterances, nuances of expression and subtleties of meaning which don't really emerge until late adolescence. The adult variety of language is a long time coming.[5]

That aside, though, it's still the very young whose neurological mechanisms are fine-tuned for its early fast growth, and who have to get the thing going, and the implication of this is that spoken language came about as an adaptation that was needed at the start of life – that it has survival value for infants.

This might sound an unlikely explanation if applied to children in today's protective, westernized societies. Yet even now, the young of our species are born helpless, vulnerable and dependent on those around for their every need, and it will be many years before they can fend for themselves. Every new-born risks being confronted by adoring incompetents, so communicating with those who care for them is central to their well-being. Indeed it's easy to overlook how often infants themselves are the ones who actually initiate communication, but they do, from their birth-cry onwards. They arrive with a powerful drive to maximize their chances, and they do this by the only means possible – attracting attention, getting what they want, and seeking to make sense of everything they hear and see around them. Therein lies safety.

What helps, of course, is that there's a natural interplay between infants' needs, their desires and capabilities, and the responses of those caring for them. Infants soon learn to shape the sounds they make, turning babble into syllables, words and phrases – using this ability to forge the relationships with carers that will keep them alive.

From their earliest days infants also tap into anything which will help them understand what they hear, see and feel. They learn to recognize what's familiar, begin to explore what's new, and slowly find their feet socially. Throughout these early years they gradually increase their ability to focus attention for longer periods of time. And all the while, behind the scenes, these activities are creating a multitude of vital neurological pathways in diverse regions of the brain - fostering those abilities which supply the crucial ingredients for the understanding and use of spoken language.[6]

Although to begin with, adult care-givers may well be looking ahead to the usefulness of words and sentences, growing infants themselves are blissfully unaware of what lies ahead. For them, any utterance and understanding is an instant, spontaneous necessity and pleasure that gets results. Infants aren't aiming for the mature form of spoken language as an objective - any more than ancestral species would have been striving to reach the complex form that we recognize and use today.

So where's the evidence?
Some may doubt the legitimacy of suggesting a parallel between what enables present-day child language to develop and what happened in distant prehistory, yet they'd probably accept without question that light and moisture made trees grow then, just as they do now.

So an appendix (Appendix 1) is offered at the end of the book which briefly describes the factors which, stage by stage, make spoken language grow today. It is presented in tandem with the book's chapters, allowing a comparison to be made with the processes described in the story.

What's really relevant is that spoken language doesn't grow by itself, any more than children will grow by themselves – they need food. During the first two or three years of life it's vital that care-givers recognize and respond to infants' vocal activities and efforts. Interactions that feed communication, ultimately transforming a simple birth-cry into spoken language are often taken for granted, yet it is these which could throw light on how it evolved.

I believe that it is reasonable to suppose that ancestral species were able to adapt and develop their communication according to principles similar to those underpinning spoken language development today: the necessary interactions of the moment put their system under pressure, and supported by abilities that were coincidentally developing alongside, progress was possible - helpful adaptations were made.

We evolved from a social primate species, and all down the generations, individuals were relating to each other, and trying to get to grips with their world.

And the world those ancestral species inhabited was often a very savage world indeed.

Throughout many thousands of years hominin families were at the mercy of animals who sought them out as prey, and they repeatedly had to face hardships caused by the climate – the way it affected the environment, and what they could find to eat. They responded by developing different strategies and skills, and because they were species that lived in social groups, that involved communication too.

Lifestyles altered, and inevitably and always, at the sharpest end of hominin existence were their vulnerable young. Like the young of any species, they were just as committed to staying alive as the adults were. So, with the neurological flexibility of youth on their side, it was *their* innovations[7] which sparked significant changes in the communication systems they'd inherited.

However, the question of evidence for such a claim is bound to be a difficult one. There's a great wealth of academic literature on the subject of language origins, provided by the highest authorities in their fields[8] – work by anthropologists, neuroscientists, psycholinguists, primatologists, computational linguists – the awesome list goes on – yet mysteries remain. At the individual level – the place where something new started to develop –

what happened? *When* did it happen? And *how* did it happen?

(*Where* it happened is, fortunately, less of a problem. Although there's still debate about when the various migrations out of Africa occurred, that continent does look like a reliable candidate for providing our most ancient mother-tongue. Research[9] carried out on 504 world languages found that those with the most sound 'families' (phonemes) were spoken in Africa; those with least in places colonised in recent human history - South America and tropical islands in the Pacific. This follows just the same pattern as human genetic diversity: modern humans emerged in Africa about 200,000 years ago, and it is in Africa that there is the greatest genetic diversity.)

What this book sets out to show then, is that in the prehistory of spoken language, there were situations which could have presented problems for the young, from infancy to adolescence that only *enhanced* communication skills could solve. It suggests how some of the familiar features of spoken language may have emerged to cope. It is a narrative offering a series of scenarios that begins with the hominins who ventured out of the forests onto a different, more open landscape, and accompanies those who succeeded them, until the emergence of our own species, *Homo sapiens*.

Spoken language, even in its earliest forms, has to be *about* something in the life of the speakers, about how they feel, what they need to express. And that's why this book is a story – why individuals and families are the main characters, not language itself.

As each ancestral line was replaced by, or evolved into its successor, advances in abilities can be deduced (albeit often tentatively) from fossilized bones, artefacts, the debris of its lifestyle and the locations where they were found. And although the proposition here is that infants were the original driving force, just what they were able to achieve (if anything) was restricted by the level the adults of each *species* had reached. They could only push out the boundaries they'd inherited. Progress came in stages.

And spoken language doesn't exist in isolation - it weaves itself around all the things we do, so the story draws on those advances in cognition and changes in behaviour which have been generally accepted by authorities on human evolution.

However, assertions about the past are often difficult to prove, and even the different processes by which adaptations arise and establish themselves are the subject of debate.[10] I therefore freely acknowledge that in using my imagination to bring this story to life I am treading a risky path. But the intention here is to explore ideas – to show possibilities – and to do so from a new perspective.

For the fact is that we *do* talk – and what can't be disputed is that many thousands of years ago ancestral humans changed their lifestyles, then changed them again, and changed them again. Implicit in their drive to survive was a communication system, which also changed. Through the heat and the cold, the wet and the dry, they and their offspring adapted to live in many landscapes. Maybe, somewhere in the struggle of their days it will be possible to detect the echoes of our elusive and forgotten first words.

So this is why and how I think spoken language came about, and as I said before, the story begins in a tree...

CHAPTER 1

Bipedalism – Now the Bad News

Australopithecus   afarensis…3.6 million years ago.[1]

The hillside trees and lowland thickets, normally alive with the activities of small birds, slowly fell silent. Down on the lowest slopes the browsing animals lifted their heads, twitching their ears and nostrils. When the smell came, carried on the edge of the hot breeze, they turned and began moving, gathering speed as the land opened out.

In one of the taller upland trees, a group of hominins had also stopped feeding. The largest male, weighing around 45 kg, and perhaps a metre and a half in height, had raised himself up, observing the change in behaviour – the way the scattered animals had closed up, leaving together in their particular small herds. He too drew in his breath, sniffing, and looking round towards the mountain range beyond the hills. The kudu and the waterbuck, the buffalo and the monkeys, all of them were on the move.

He let out the "wraaa" call of uncertainty, repeating it as he shifted through the branches. The other males began matching the sound, and then the whole troop was swinging down. Two females had young. One of the infants was alerted when he realised that the fruit gathering had stopped, and had scrambled through the canopy to lodge on his mother's back. The other had been suckling, so simply tightened his grip on his mother's skin.

Down on the ground the troop continued their calling - the apprehension of the big male transmitting itself to all of them. Keeping close, but jostling for position to try and find a better opening to see through the trees, they searched for the source of the smell.

From their throats the barks came faster. Fire they recognised. It was an occasional occurrence, and though a threat to hominins, when it was far away they could move fast enough to get out of its path.

But this wasn't quite like fire.

The barks became shrill screams and agitation exploded into action as the hominins' dark forms broke from the shelter of the trees to create their own small clouds of dust, following the other animals into more open country.

The lowland was an extensive area dotted with bushes and a few sparse areas of woodland. When they were out foraging the hominins quartered the land using these groves of trees as markers, because apart from the leaves and seasonal fruit, the trees also provided a refuge, and somewhere to sleep, so remembering the location was useful.

Now they paid scant attention to their whereabouts, and the group kept up its intense pace until they were well away from the hills. They covered the ground on all fours, using the knuckles of their slender hands to propel themselves in a side-long, loping run. They kept together, even though the females had young and might have fallen behind, except that they were more lightly built and accustomed to travelling quickly when the need arose.

Eventually they slowed, and their progress became a bent and ungainly walk. The hominins would have to be more watchful now, and a more upright posture helped. Walking normally consisted of a wide-based stride, and with their arched feet and long toes, the Afarensis were bi-pedal, but it was a movement that lacked the easy grace which still swung them through the forest canopy.

From time to time they glanced back at the mountain range, and whatever had caused the acrid smell filling the air, it was still creeping after them with a noise like thunder that seemed even to come from underfoot. From the volcano a plume of smoke rose into the sky, immense and dark. The hominins pressed on, focused only on getting further away, but as night fell they needed to search for trees. Finally they could make nests and rest in the familiarity of branches.

When they awoke, a pale film of ash covered everything. Hungry and inexperienced, the young hominin tore at a nearby leaf and put it in his mouth. In an instant, he was spitting and shaking his head to be rid of it, letting out whimpers of distress, and his mother pulled him close to calm him. She studied the leaves and brushed the dust off with the tip of a finger, then smelt them. She knew they would be inedible.

She swung down, giving half-spitting warning calls as she went. The tree would not supply food, and there were still disturbing sounds in the distance as well as the pervasive smell.

The hominin group continued south-west through the following day. Occasionally a particular leaf-shape growing through grasses indicated the presence underground of roots which could be eaten, and they stopped and dug down for them using fingers, sticks and any sharp stones they could find. The danger did seem to be receding, so they could resume walking now, and the older infant let go of his mother to trail beside her.

The younger one still needed to be carried. He had long strong arms and used them well to find his way through the canopy, but his first attempts at standing and walking would be tentative. In the trees, if need be, he could travel slung underneath his mother's stomach, but if she was walking, as now, he could only lodge on her back. From there, however, he could see where the various individuals went, and what they were doing. Like them, his face was large and flat, sloping forward beneath his nose to a narrow mouth. His cheekbones were prominent, since the muscles needed for chewing were attached there and were large and powerful. His eyes darted everywhere, alert to those around him, learning what they did to survive.

~~~~~~~~

The ancestors of the hominin group had enjoyed a history of familiarity with the close green forest environment which had left them at ease with the demands of moving about within it. They had interpreted its moods and the comings and goings of its other inhabitants. But when the forest grew thinner it could no longer supply a localised and reliable source of food. At its edge and beyond, though, alternatives could be found, down where the light allowed other kinds of plants to thrive. So the Afarensis had ventured out and discovered what was available - and what else was also satisfying its hunger in the grass and behind the thickets. They'd found that standing up made it easier to view the expanse of the lowland vegetation and its accompanying predators. Gradually they adjusted to the distance confronting
~~~~~~~~

them, and gradually walking became a better way of moving about.

They were exploiting a mosaic of habitats: thick forest, woodland areas here and there, and now the grassy plains. All tugged at their curiosity, drawing them little by little towards new ways of foraging. If keeping their sights on faraway trees whose blossoms were familiar meant staying upright to reach them, then they stretched their legs to the uttermost and imperceptibly the extra effort grew less. But walking wasn't just a physical adaptation. Behind the scenes the brain was having to make room for a host of new perceptions - exploration of this varied landscape presented sights, sounds, smells and sensations which had created new responses.

Occasionally, a new response could arise from the demands of just a single extraordinary experience.

~~~~~~~~

Out on the plain the various small grazing and browsing herds had continued to form into bigger groups and were still on the move, though more steadily now. Occasionally, below the drumming of their hooves, the hominins could still detect deeper groans, and they would turn to look in the direction of the sound, and there, away to the north, the smoke hung against a lowering sky. Although its violence was abating, from time to time the volcano still threw out ash, and wherever they walked, the hominins were leaving tracks in the thick dry dust, adding their prints to those of the animals.

The older of the infants kept up with the adults until they'd crossed a depression in the ground
~~~~~~~~

where a river sometimes flowed. The Afarensis could sustain this pattern of walking interspersed with feeding over considerable distances - perhaps five or six kilometres - but for a youngster, achieving balance, learning to coordinate all the necessary movements, pacing himself - these were skills he was still in the early stages of mastering. Also, he was desperate with hunger. Unable to extract starch from the tough fibrous tubers as quickly as the adults, he was already weak. He could tear at leaves using canine teeth, and at four years old, he had the strong grinding molars and premolars he would need to manage whatever food the hominins might find. But sustained chewing required energy, and this was running low.

His mother, like the three other females, was now some way ahead in the bushes, searching for berries. The infant sat himself down at the edge of the depression, turning stones and dried leaves in a listless search for anything which might be edible.

Suddenly he was distracted. Huge drops of rain began making craters in the grey dust. A gradual crescendo of sputtering turned itself into a deluge, swirling round the small figure on the ground, soaking his fur. He struggled to his feet, overwhelmed by yet another strange occurrence. At a distance, the group abandoned their foraging, forced to move again, ready as always to make for the protection of trees. When the infant's mother cast about to find him he was out of sight and range of her urgent calls, and his own whimpering and shrill screams of fright were drowned by the din of rain beating on the leaf litter and the hard ground.

If a tree branch had been nearby, the deep-seated urge to climb would have come to his rescue – but although he was trying to stand in an effort to see the familiar shapes of his group, the rain defeated him, and his legs gave way. He began knuckle-walking with no sense of which way to go, until overwhelmed by fear the infant hominin sank onto the ground again. He was panting and filled with tension, so that when he opened his mouth it was wide and his lips were tight. The sound was prolonged and in those fractions of a second the thick muscles in his cheeks gave it added resonance.

'eeaaagh!'

The sound repeated itself over and over.

'eeaaaagh…eeaaaagh!'

It carried through the surging rain, and recognising his voice within this strange cry, the infant's mother straightened up, homing in on the sound, then came for him, gathering him up in her long arms.

Sheltering with the group in the lee of bushes, she sat trying to soothe him.

~~~~~~~~

Perhaps she cradled him in the curve of her body, gently rocking him. Such a movement would reflect the way tree branches swayed in the breeze, a familiar sensation that might lend its calming effect to the Afarensis when they fled to safety in the canopy or settled to sleep at night, just as it had to their tree-dwelling predecessors.

Now however they were dealing with an environment where trees had parted company. Escape wasn't always possible, and with less cover Afarensis families had to be much more careful to conceal themselves. A crying infant was an instant invitation to predators, so the females would have
~~~~~~~~

needed ways of pacifying them, of calming their cries.

Whatever its origins, and whenever in our evolution it developed, the rocking and moving of infants is something that occurs in all human cultures. It is so deeply ingrained that we do it instinctively to calm and quieten a fretful baby. Traditional rocking cradles have lulled countless generations of babies to sleep. But the practice confers additional, hidden and more subtle benefits.

A tiny mechanism deep in the brain is stimulated during moving and rocking, and this is the vestibular system. Intriguingly it is closely involved in maintaining the upright posture we adopt when we walk, so moving infants in such a way primes the brain for when they take their first steps.[2]

The species that went on to establish walking as their preferred means of travel would develop a host of cognitive skills necessary for exploring and exploiting new environments. And if language would ultimately draw on those skills – tapping into those areas of the brain which were growing - then becoming bipedal was fertile ground for spoken language. The Afarensis were the first to venture away from the forests, so maybe recapturing the tranquillity of trees was an additional small contribution to its complex origins.

Where they roamed is a part of Africa known as the Afar Depression – it's the area which has given them their name – and in a few places they left something of themselves behind. Nothing much, and mostly in the Great Rift Valley, that long scar curving down the eastern side of Africa. There, in the section where the valley runs north towards the Gulf of Aden, a few bones have been unearthed.

But at Laetoli,[3] about half way down its length, the Afarensis left footprints. They were made by two adults and a younger hominin, and they were all walking. The imprints were left in volcanic ash, set like concrete by the rainstorm which had followed. Alongside were the hoof prints of the animals which, like them, were fleeing from the eruption of Mt. Sadiman.

Such proof that this species walked represents more than just a physical adaptation, though; walking had extended the environments in which they could survive, and a range of different skills would arise as a consequence. In the Afarensis, the primate brain would have been reorganising itself.

And whilst being bipedal might be proving an advantage for Afarensis adults, the youngest hominins faced considerable risk compared with the infants of their predecessors, when forests covered the land. Until they were competent walkers they could be carried during forays, but once they were weaned and obliged to search for food themselves, care-giving adults might travel faster and further – disappearing into the dappled distance - and that was when the crunch came.

The Afarensis had inherited a way of communicating formed by a lifestyle in the trees. Like the birdsong and the humming of the insects, it was an integral part of the teeming forest harmony. Their expressive calls, attitudes of body, drumming on the base of trees, had all served them well. They would have had to be adept at sifting out what was significant – be it the nuances in the sound of their voices, or the information conveyed by their visible signals. And while the Afarensis hovered between the forest and the woodland perimeter, there was probably no great pressure on their system forcing it to change. But as they ventured out onto the grasslands something else would happen. Where was the predictable background of sounds that characterised dense forests? Away from the sheltering canopy, wouldn't their own calls come over differently?

As for infants, they were literally small voices crying in the wilderness, whose survival depended on getting themselves heard and responded to quickly. Not that they were unique in this - all young mammals use a 'separation cry' to alert their mothers when they feel endangered. But an increase in the frequency of dangerous situations and greater extremes of physical tension could alter the characteristics of an infant's cry on those occasions. For hominin mothers, something which alerted them more effectively also improved their offsprings' chances of being quickly found, and in those families where the innovation caught on, more infants would go on to breed. Where would we be if our infant ancestors had been eaten?

The seedbed for spoken language ...
- An altered environment was provoking different vocal activity.
- Exploring was putting pressure on cognitive abilities.

CHAPTER 2

Diet and Exercise

Australopithecus afarensis (continued)...3.0 million years ago.

The descendants of the group which had fled the fumes and ash from the volcano had migrated through the years and the thousands of years, inevitably adjusting as the climate exerted its influence over the landscape. As each changing habitat merged into its neighbour, the hominins were coping and progressing, cognitively as well as physically.

They had amassed experience of broad areas of grassland intermingled with thickets and patches of woodland, and these, depending on altitude and aspect, were interspersed with larger stretches of forest. There were densely clothed hillsides, rivers cutting through from the highlands, and in low-lying regions, there were lakes and marshlands. The whims of the weather - daily or by season, in a lifetime or many lifetimes - added further twists to the routes which the Afarensis followed, and all the while it was the brain's capacity to respond and direct behaviour which allowed the species to survive.

~~~~~~~~

Now a family group of about twenty individuals of varying ages was slowly making its way across a dry grassland, heading towards an outline of trees – an indication of the damper ground which supported vegetation alongside the course of a river. For the moment the Afarensis were resting
~~~~~~~~

under an acacia tree. It was shady, and they were examining the bones from what, some weeks before, had been a leopard kill draped on a branch. On route to the river they would look for the underground rhizomes of some of the grassland plants, and though these were easily uncovered they weren't easy to eat. With the help of one or two of the heavier bones, however, the hard bulb could be smashed and digestion made easier.

The face of the dominant male had been placid, his lips closed, but now he stood up and his lower lip dropped showing the pink of his gums. He had been food-grunting during his selection of a bone, and the others were watching him.[1]

'uuh…tuhtuhtuh….'

He was striking his tongue against the back of his teeth, and the sound was taken up as the hominins moved out across the grassland. Youngsters who had been playing under the acacia quickly followed where the adults were heading, recognising the sound. It was a noise made in the mouth when the tongue pushed roots against incisor teeth – they knew what kind of plant they were after.

The group separated into smaller clusters of individuals, and where there were females with young, the calls were sometimes interspersed with a *'hoo'* sound, answered by their infants. This was part of their general repertoire, but now the Afarensis were using it to replace the high-pitched side-scratching (a relic of the forest-dwelling era) which signalled readiness to travel. In the open, it was their voices which carried better, and which were now helping to keep everyone on the move.

A small group of juveniles who had been play-fighting, carried on their noisy game as they moved, drawing a cautionary bark from an older male. As in the past, warnings and aggression had always needed to be loud, but many expressions used when individuals were near each another, like panting, lip-smacking and teeth-clacking, hadn't ever needed to carry far and were voiceless. In a more open environment, however, things were different.

Strategies for maintaining group cohesion had developed out of necessity. In this varied assortment of habitats there was a varied assortment of opportunities, and danger everywhere. It was no longer safe to go looking for food alone as it had been in the past. The old (who had knowledge of where certain foods could be found) and the young (who struggled to keep up) needed protection; staying together was better all round. And it was communication that was helping them do this.

On the move they kept each other well in view. With their hands free, information passed through broad gestures, supplementing calls or maybe supplemented by them. They were also alert to the way a facial expression might change. Walking upright meant faces were usually clearly visible – relaxation, distress, aggression, fear - any emotion was instantly evident, so the hominins paid more attention. The small infants, trailing alongside the females, constantly turned to whoever was nearby. Their range of vision was restricted and if there was danger, they had to find out where it lay, and they did this by watching faces. If they could detect which way the adults were looking they'd invented an early warning system for themselves.[2]

Here in the grass, having checked and rechecked that the area was safe, the Afarensis were quickly focused on the task in hand. The more mature young males, around 15 years old, soon formed a scouting party ahead of the rest. They had an agenda other than rhizomes: they were after the brown lizards that sunned themselves on rocks. Catching them was reasonably easy because the reptiles were large enough to grab, but unless they were approached swiftly the faint tremors in the earth caused by the approaching hominins would send the lizards scuttling down the nearest crack.

One of the young males let out an excited pant-hoot of triumph, straightening up and displaying the writhing body of the lizard in his hand. Still calling, he dashed it against the rock and began tearing at its flesh with his teeth. His tongue pulled at chunks of the meat, moving it against the hard ridges of his palate, separating bones to be spat out, and then his jaws worked it until the back of his tongue shifted the lumps for him to swallow.

Hearing his shout, one of the females paused from digging at the root she had found, looking towards the male, and then returning to her task. She knew what he'd caught. It was a combination of information – the way he'd been moving, and the way his call altered in anticipation of eating it. She wouldn't need to beg from him, though. Small grubs and other insects often lived close to the underground food, and by careful scrutiny of the earth around she would certainly find enough to eat. Eating for her was a more delicate matter; lips closed on the morsels ensuring that nothing escaped, and quick flicks of her tongue whipped them behind her teeth where they were crushed.

Nearby, other females and three or four of the small infants were doing the same. From time to time, when something new had been caught, picked or dug up, particular sounds floated on the air like the chattering of the bush birds.

~~~~~~~~

The food-sounds had begun just as all hominin vocalisations had done – as an expression of some emotion. Excitement, puzzlement, rage – whatever they felt was conveyed as much in the sounds they made as in the explicit body movements which accompanied them. Like the chimpanzees and macaques, their calls told if food was good or bad. So satisfaction would often provoke vocal activity, but the innovation which the Afarensis were introducing now was the result of their coping – increasingly well – with so many new and different foodstuffs.[3]

It was, however, the infants who would be at the forefront of the process. As with the bipedalism issue, when it came to eating, they'd got a very raw deal indeed. They were suckled just as their tree-dwelling ancestors had been, but what happened when it came time for weaning? Instead of soft fruits and tender flowers, the menu contained a host of ingredients so uncompromising that they forced evolutionary change on even the teeth.[4]

The Afarensis had a diet which ranged from reptiles to rodents, soft fruit to seeds, tubers to leaves and palm nuts to bush piglets.[5] Sometimes considerable time and effort was needed to chew and manoeuvre edible items in the mouth, so what they ate exercised lips, tongue, teeth, jaws and cheeks in challenging ways, and heightened sensations of texture and shape, as well as flavour.

Maybe to start with, Afarensis mothers took a leaf out of another bush and chewed the tough stuff
~~~~~~~~

themselves before offering it to their infants. But this would only be a temporary stage; sooner or later, infant hominins would have to tackle the problems of difficult food themselves.

To manage at all, infants already arrived with some useful inherited adaptations, so their oral muscles would gradually find their way round the lumpy bits, the gristle, the squashy parts and the bone. It was hard work and it took time before they became adept. But thus sensitised, and obliged to be strong and more versatile, the oral muscles were then available for increasing the range of sounds it was possible to make[6] – given the opportunity.

And of course, once hunger was satisfied, infants would engage in just the sort of boisterous play that is typical of young mammals – noisier than adults, and an obvious chance for those oral muscles to experiment with existing sounds and enjoy the feel and effect of new ones.

Even the face-watching, unconscious though it was, would make a contribution. It was a skill the Afarensis shared with the chimpanzees, who sometimes adopted it when trying to discover the focus of another's interest, and such a habit would usefully spill into games. The by-product was that an infant brain could absorb information about the way the face moved when playmates vocalised - the changes in shape which accompanied different sounds. If vocal variations conveyed something more quickly, there was the chance they might spread among playmates and linger, creeping seamlessly into the adult calls the new generation would go on to make. They might even be picked up by adults.

Chimpanzees have demonstrated this 'bottom-up' approach – it's known that young ones have passed on new feeding techniques to their elders.

If older kin did indeed pick up new vocal expressions – continuing to learn beyond the period of infancy – then their behaviour would also have resembled that of some birds. Those which spread themselves in a favoured habitat, like the Afarensis were doing, carried on adding elements to their songs for longer than those species which tended to stay put[7] · birds did this through flight, the Afarensis through walking. And as with any physical activity, where practice and a little maturity improved coordination, variations could establish, rather than fading away.

Taking advantage of food sounds that communicated their finds, a group might forage just a little more easily and a little more successfully.

~~~~~~~~

There was an urge to move on. The expanse of grass in which the Afarensis group had been feeding yielded nothing more, and the hominins scrutinised the surrounding landscape before continuing across the bush land towards a dark outline of trees.

Already that day they had covered a distance of about 7 kilometres - a journey which would have represented the limit of Afarensis forays during the early period of their existence, but by now they had grown used to long treks.

It was hot, and as in the past, the Afarensis went by way of copses offering shade. They had fallen silent, responding mainly to signals given out by facial expression and posture. The leading male
~~~~~~~~

was still carrying his bone, and this he brandished from time to time in much the same way that the forest apes used leafy branches to get their families to follow them. But mainly they moved with care, and listened.

Insects flew up as they walked, and when the Afarensis disturbed a francolin – a slow, partridge-like bird - its frantic scrabble to get away and crescendo of squawks caused an answering commotion of screams and barks. The hominins settled down again, the urge to vocalise fading as they resumed paying attention to their surroundings. Hints of a predator's presence were often far more subtle than those of the fat and noisy bird.

And it was the movement of a shadow which drew a high-pitched string of sounds from one of the youngsters. Sharp-eyed, he had recognised the shape and immediately made a call identifying the eagle. It had spotted the hominins from its perch in one of the distant trees behind them.

Like the agile vervet monkeys, the Afarensis could tell others of particular dangers or predators by using specific calls;[8] now, having more sounds at their disposal they could fine-tune that ability – and extend it. They had the hazards of woodlands, bush and grassland to watch out for.

The Afarensis group turned on the huge bird, yelling and flapping their arms and it soared away, and while an eagle couldn't have taken an adult, infants were easy pickings. The signal had alerted everyone, and the appropriate response had kept the little ones safe.

The vegetation thickened as the Afarensis drew closer to the river and its wide border of trees. They had been travelling as a band, but now they had to separate a little and one of the juvenile females was making her way alone through deciduous bushes. Suddenly she paused, stiffening, cocking her head to one side and staring intently at the ground beneath a small shrub ahead of her. A movement in the leaf litter caused a soft rustle. The female waited. Again came the faint vibration – not as light as a shrew, different. Long, somehow.

The snake was small, and could have killed her. The young female hadn't observed it slither into the depths of the shrub, and it was simply her stillness that had protected her, giving the snake time to deal with the threat by retreating. After a moment or two she relaxed, uncertain what had caused the leaves to tremble.

During the month or so that the Afarensis remained in the vicinity, however, curiosity enticed her back to the shrub from time to time, and she watched, hopeful there might be a meal to be had.

Seeing the creature emerge one day, sleek and with a vibrant yellow and purple-black skin, the female instinctively froze; this was no meal. Without a nearby tree her only option was to remain where she was. Tense and fearful, she waited for it to go, but then caught sight of one of the fierce little cats which lived in the trees preparing to stalk the snake. The cat approached, low and slow, but the snake's darting tongue picked up its scent. It reared up out of the leaves, hissing and swaying, breaking the cat's concentration. When the cat turned tail, and the snake too had safely vanished, the female opened her mouth, mimicking its awful gape.

'hhhhaaa……" she hissed, *"hhhhaaa…'"*

She had made the sound long, like the snake. The female turned, the sound becoming a wisp of information that combined itself with the image which her mind would retain of the scene. This capacity to imitate was proving to be rather useful.

~~~~~~~~

In times past, imitation may well have included watching and copying the ways foodstuffs were dealt with – actions most obviously involving the hands. There were cells in the brain - 'mirror neurons'[9] which sprang to life when another's grasping movements were observed, and there was clearly a benefit to be gained by learning feeding skills from other members of a group. But foodstuffs hadn't stayed the same.   Far more dexterity was needed, and there was far more work for the muscles of lips tongue and jaws. In the brain, if it was organised as it is in us today, the centre which controls the hands is close to the area dealing with the mouth. So neurons busy reacting to moving fingers might well influence neurons alongside, registering what the oral muscles had to do too. Copying how someone gnawed at a root, or shredded a stem was valuable – the 'mirror' process was extending its role. But the muscles of lips, tongue and jaw were going yet further. Copying the sounds they made was also valuable.

Once calls of all kinds began to contain more sounds, therefore, the instinctive answering habits of mothers and young could make the most of these mirror neurons. Bipedalism was expanding the kind of situations where contact calling was needed, so when the young raised their voices, Afarensis mothers could reply with the same sounds they were hearing from their infants. It might happen again and again, because, like other primates, the young depended on their mothers for
~~~~~~~~

many years. Particular calls were an ideal way to reassure them,   helping them to find each other when grasses were tall or thickets dense. A habit of vocal imitation had survival value.

What would also have survival value though, would be to prolong the copying habit beyond early infancy and beyond simple reassurance. If adult calls were conveying more by dint of their gathered experiences, then the sooner the young also used them themselves the better. Their own mirror systems would give them a start as would the longer, bird-like learning period they were developing. But imitation itself might need a boost, and it's quite possible it had obtained that through another aspect of the Afarensis lifestyle.

Searching out food in the changed environments had demanded a capacity to match; something new, tentatively tasted and satisfying, had to be found again. So its appearance was important, and recognising when one thing looked the same as another was essential. Visual matching had helped when it came to predators, but so had auditory matching – recognising footfalls, growls and howls or bird calls that sent out warnings - these demanded urgent understanding of what was the same. So when it came to the imitation of their own Afarensis vocal sounds, auditory matching could step in again and join forces with the mirror neurons. Copying each other would prove to have enormous significance as time went by.

An individual lucky enough to have an aptitude for a particular skill could also pass it on. The juvenile female, still receptive and learning from her encounter with the snake, would, of course, be ready to mate quite soon. If successful she could bestow on her offspring not only better than average hearing, but also an ability to make valuable connections. Like her, they'd learn to distinguish what was significant from noise that could be regarded as background, and so could isolate for attention anything unusual their ears picked out of the busy surroundings. Other senses would back that up – was the sound uncharacteristic for the landscape they were in? Then curiosity would get to the bottom of what made it, past experience could evaluate it, and the conclusion would pass into their personal stores of perceptions. If, like her, they could reinforce the memory with another detail – a spontaneous reaction expressed in sound – they were just a little better equipped for next time.

The Afarensis had had a multitude of situations to deal with, and listening intently had been utterly imperative. What they heard around them had an array of subtle qualities that helped them to differentiate between the creatures making the sounds, and even to interpret their intentions or condition. So something rasping or soft might be the stealthy preparation for a swift and lethal pounce, a faint or quiet call might be a weak or distant animal, the sharp and sudden treetop clatter might be the timely warning of an approaching predator, signalled by the curved-billed ibis.

It was this necessary embellishment to the Afarensis' listening skills which underpinned their own ability to create sounds with different qualities. With hearing on full alert they could detect and understand the variations in sounds that each of them uttered. And with a wider repertoire playing on their lips and an ability to imitate, any helpful variations would tend to stick. The Afarensis remembered what their own distinct calls told them, associating the calls both with the food or animals in question and with the best means of dealing with them.

Listening, along with observing the behaviour of animals was an increasingly essential activity because the lifestyle demanded it. Whenever they left the cover of the trees they were as exposed as any of the herd animals and like them they developed a sense of when prowling carnivores were about to attack; they picked up on small changes and understood their implications. With each other too they listened, noted posture and facial expression and picked up inklings about what each might do next.

~~~~~~~~

The group nearing the band of trees along the river bank were listening, but not, as it happened, to each other. They were also watching, but again, the focus of attention was elsewhere, on something going on in the topmost branches. It was monkeys. A large troop was swinging through the trees, moving along parallel with the river. The commotion above contributed to the hominins' excitement, and although some individuals were more capable of suppressing the tendency to make food-calls when following prey alone, being together meant that anticipation, with its accompanying clamour, was infectious and the air was filled with screams, hoots and barks. Complete control of vocal activity would take time and effort to achieve, but it was making a start.

Infants might well be the first to suffer if their vocalisations drew unwelcome attention to themselves as their families travelled from place to
~~~~~~~~

place. So if keeping quiet was also a survival mechanism, the young had the most powerful incentive for learning how to do it.

Now was the time for action, though. Under the trees the hominins spread out, each one intent on identifying any monkey showing potential as a target: old, injured, or infant on its own. When selections were made the hominins clustered again, as they tended to do when cooperation made success more likely, drawn by drumming, branch-waving and loud calls. The monkeys were chased and driven until some hunts had succeeded, and the hominins settled in nearby trees to feed. Nests were made, and they passed the night there, waking at dawn when the birds broke the stillness – a reminder, if one were needed, of another reason why they'd come.

It was breeding season for many of the birds, and their eggs were there for the taking. The meat from the colobus monkeys had been a good helping of protein but took hours to digest, whereas raiding nests was considerably more energy-efficient[10] - shells were swiftly broken into and this protein didn't even need chewing. All the better if the eggs were large.

Down at the river's edge the Afarensis crouched to drink, sucking water from handfuls of the moss-like vegetation which grew in shady hollows. Fearful of buffalos, they were jittery, constantly cocking an ear for shudders in the ground that might tell of their approach, on the look-out for the shaking of leaves on nearby banks. But they were also checking for the whereabouts of a particular species of heron. Its nest, an untidy collection of sticks, was always on the lower branches of a bank-side tree, and its eggs were big. The hominins had noted a wide mudflat on a bend in the river, which was typical of the sort of places such birds liked to fish.

The group stood up, refreshed, and continued casting about for any sign of the herons. When one of the hominins spotted the nest he caught the gaze of others, turning his head in that direction. He was teeth-clacking - something often done during enjoyable rough-and tumbles, but now it imitated exactly the furious beak-clattering made by the herons if they were disturbed.

At the water's edge the five or six infants stopped their inquisitive scrambling, about to learn something new. They too focussed their attention where the adults were looking. The raid would have to be done quietly. Scaring the female heron off her newly-laid eggs could only be attempted while her mate was intent on fishing, and it required one hominin to be within reach of the eggs while another kept the female away from them.

Excitement was threatening to break out again. The Afarensis males made moves towards the females, baring their teeth in an open grin.

'hheh…hheh'

It was a warning to back off, and the soft sound had the desired effect. Taking their infants they retreated quietly into the woods, while two of the males went ahead of the rest, keeping under cover of vegetation and working their way cautiously towards the nest. One carried a long stick which he was stripping of its lower twigs. He would use it to try and draw branches nearer if the nest was hard to reach.

He was within inches, and the sitting bird was rising, clacking in alarm. However, obscured by branches overhanging the mudflat, the heron's mate had indeed been fishing, but was already returning. Unaware, the hominin saw his moment to strike and lunged at the female - a costly mistake. The ensuing attack by both birds was vicious.

Given time, hominins waiting at a distance would develop a particular call, understood by those doing the stalking - a warning that the heron doing the fishing had taken flight and was coming back.

For the present, though, the hominin nursed his wounds and the group made do with smaller eggs, snatched from the nests of waterfowl hidden amongst the reeds under the river bank. There would be other attempts, and other years, because the Afarensis followed the seasons. Provided they ranged far enough, there was food to be had, and they had the skills and stamina to exploit it.

~~~~~~~~

Throughout their history there had been periods when torrential rains had encouraged the forests to grow, and the river had often burst its banks, flooding into the flat valley through which it flowed. Then, when the forests dwindled and the river ran low, new generations of hominins pursued it downstream. If that failed, they foraged among the reed beds of the vast lake in the middle of the lowland,[11] until that too shrank and forced them on. Eventually, perhaps, their descendants might have gone so far north as to reach the sea, with its coastal marshes and tidal pools, and at every step of the way they had pushed the boundaries of what they could eat and how they could deal with the hazards of obtaining it.

In many respects they differed little from their tree-dwelling ancestors and cousins.[12] But
~~~~~~~~

bipedalism implied more than just walking on two instead of four legs. It was what went on inside their heads that really counted. Areas of the brain which were involved in the actions and sensations of eating, of calling, listening, observing, imitating, remembering – all these were at the forefront of the Afarensis' capacity to survive. The grey matter was being kept busy; cells neighbouring those areas most in use - or distant but already associated - were being warmed up. They would be the areas for the brain to recruit if the push came for further development, and hominin communication would tap into all of them.[13]

<u>The seedbed for spoken language…</u>

- More agile muscles made variations in vowels and consonants possible.

- Situations strengthened the ability to match and imitate.

- The environment demanded keener listening skills and the capacity to understand the implications of sounds heard.

CHAPTER 3

Getting Personal

Homo habilis…2.4 million years ago.

If the long hard lifestyle of the Afarensis had indeed sown some of the seeds for spoken language, then the pressure would have to increase - things would have to get worse before the first shoots could get any bigger.

And of course things did get worse.

Global temperatures had frequently fluctuated widely, but now the polar ice sheets were slowly and inexorably drawing moisture away even from the hot equatorial regions of the world where this story takes place.[1] There could still be cycles of heavy rainfall, followed by drought, either of which might last many thousands of years. But through the whole length of the period between 2 and 3 million years ago the trend was always away from the warm, wet climate in which the forests and woodlands had flourished. In this cooler, drier climate, the flora and fauna would, if they could, find ways of adapting. If they couldn't, they declined and disappeared.

Maybe that was the fate of the Afarensis. By about 2.5 million years ago they seem to have bowed out. There might, of course, have been places in that increasingly arid interior where groups of them still existed, answering the privations of the time by altering stature and stance. Or maybe, hidden in the dust storms, the strategies they had adopted passed obliquely to some other lineage in the Australopithecine family. Several were successful in dealing with the capriciousness of the times, but eventually, during the next million years, their adaptations weren't enough.

Whatever actually happened, when stability began to return to the countryside, one of the bipedal species inhabiting it was *Homo habilis*. If it was these hominins who had the edge, then it would be they who had a future. In them, as with the Afarensis, evolutionary changes were prompted by what individuals had consistently encountered from day to day. The vagaries of climate had altered the environment, and such variability – even when spread through a million years – had demanded flexibility. Activities and behaviour had had to change to include a much wider range of possible responses. The driving force was always survival, and whatever senses and tactics tipped the scales in their favour, whether through sight, smell, hearing, touch – or voice – all would be stretched. And the fact is that by the end of their time, there would be *Homo habilis* remains showing the results of this pressure – skulls were larger: the brain had grown bigger.

~~~~~~~~

It was *Homo habilis* hominins who, for some time, had been occupying parts of the Great Rift Valley, and this was turning out to be a haven in the prevailing cool dry weather. In the lowlands to the east, the lack of moisture spread flora and fauna thinly, but in and around the Valley's central region, mountains reached so high that their peaks glistened white with snow and rivers cascaded down, fed by the melt-water. Wherever they flowed westwards the surrounding land offered a range of congenial habitats. Altitude influenced the
~~~~~~~~

characteristics of each one, and the Valley itself was fertile – a result of ancient volcanic activity. So as long as this volatile force was in one of its restful phases, the hominins who roamed there could satisfy their needs reliably – provided they were prepared to climb or descend, and were willing to risk exploring.

There would be one aspect of survival which would have a particular influence on their behaviour, however. Like other creatures, the Habilis were now finding themselves obliged to deliberately search for water. Rivers weren't always accessible – sometimes they flowed through rocky gorges too precipitous for hominins, but on the Valley floor there might be springs, and occasionally freshwater lakes.

One in particular was beginning to provide something more than temporary subsistence. It lay in the central section of the Valley, and was surrounded by extensive grasslands and forests. Habilis families had been exploring the uplands either side of the Valley, as well as its broad interior for millennia, generally travelling as groups of thirty to fifty, but usually maintaining a loose contact within the wider population.

This group was an extended family of mixed ages. Males were still larger than females, and both retained the long agile arms which took them with ease through the tree-tops. But here, away from cover, they were close to the water's edge and walking, sometimes stooping to collect small freshwater molluscs, and occasionally drawing together to examine evidence of other visitors to the lake. Dung was recognised by shape, size and smell - despite the sun's drying - and the characteristic pattern of prints could prompt anxiety or give reassurance that it was safe to continue.

Keeping in contact along the lakeside, the Habilis family were presenting a very different image from other primates in the vicinity. They were upright, uttering varied and distinctive calls, and arms and hands moved expressively, as if in concert with the sounds – a bonus added to communication because walking had freed up the hands.

They watched the behaviour ahead of them of storks and other wading birds, halting as one if there was a sudden flurry and the flocks rose up, wheeling, filling the air with their beating wings. All would fall silent, looking round intently, searching for whatever caused the alarm.

In this way the Habilis had enjoyed safe travelling for several days, and now, as the sun began to dip towards the horizon, they could see in the distance that a mass of vegetation encroached onto the lakeside itself. It was an undeniable attraction, promising the usual blossoms, leaves, fruits and small mammals, but with the additional advantage of water nearby. With the fading light gleaming off the surface of the lake it was still possible to see a way along its edge, and the dominant male led his group to the safety of the trees and up into the welcome canopy.

The following day confirmed the benefits of the new location. From the higher branches of trees nearest the water, the surrounding area could be kept in view, and with alarm calls alerting those down at the lake, old and young alike could forage there more freely. When they resorted to excursions into the forest, the hominins would resume their traditional ways of feeding, because they hadn't lost their old food gathering skills, they'd just added new ones.

~~~~~~~~

As far as social structure was concerned, traditional strategies had been maintained here too. The Habilis family consisted of a similar mix and size to the hominin groups which had gone before, and their lives were still dominated by the hierarchies typical of other ape families who had stayed within the forest. So there were rules of behaviour which kept them functioning successfully and which the young, as always, needed to absorb. Young Habilis hominins, however, had to be more attention-seeking than their predecessors.

One problem was still the bipedalism thing, and the stretches of open countryside that had to be crossed. Covering the distances posed no difficulties for adults, but younger hominins could run out of steam. When they flagged, they dropped behind and that meant trouble. Alarm calls and swift responses were essential.

The other difficulty was with the diet itself.

The canine teeth of some Habilis hominins were diminishing in size, as were the cheek teeth and muscles – perhaps a minor genetic mutation had affected the fibres, reducing their bulk – and this resulted in less powerful jaws. Food could no longer be chewed in a typical ape-like way. With smaller, less forwardly projecting jaws,[2] movements were less gross, more capable of variation, which was useful when it came to shifting mouthfuls around, but not so good when it came to breaking down the tough stuff.
~~~~~~~~

However, young Habilis hominins could turn such a feature to their advantage. The muscles involved were also those being used for sound-making, and inevitably Habilis vocalising would also be less ape-like. If infants and youngsters – weaned and mostly travelling within a loose family group – were casting about for ways of alerting adult hominins to the fact that they were getting left behind, or were struggling with food, then more mobile oral muscles were first in line to come to their aid. The more effective the call, the quicker they got noticed.

And Habilis adults had developed something that would really help in dealing with difficult food, because they themselves were altering how they responded to hunger. They would continue hunting the small monkeys who darted through the trees, but they also took what they could get off the carcases left behind by the large predators – and for this they were using tools to butcher them.

Released from the duty of providing anchorage for massive muscles, the bones of the skull were now free to grow, and an expanding brain took up the offer. In Habilis hominins it wasn't quite big enough to be counted as human, or small enough to still be counted as ape-sized, but there had been enough going on by way of hardships met and overcome for the brain to need more room for its store of information. And for directing the Habilis skill of making stone tools.

Observation followed by imitation followed by practice had perpetuated the skill of stripping twigs to catch termites like the chimpanzees did, so it was perhaps quite a small step for early Habilis hominins to deliberately strike one stone against another to create a tool which was sharp enough and heavy enough to break through animal carcases.

It's known that bonobos, one of our present-day great ape cousins, can make such flakes.

Not only that, bonobos' brains have developed in such a way that individuals brought up with researchers understand quite complex human verbal and symbolic communication. They vocalise,[3] and walk bipedally in a similar style to the Afarensis. But unlike them, the bonobos' habitat is the forest. There is no evidence that this species ever struck out into the open landscape, coped with a diet that produced the agility needed for complex articulation, or stretched their cognitive powers to meet the environment's far-reaching demands.

For Habilis infants, however, whose neural legacy had included adaptations to their oral musculature and whose lifestyle increased their vulnerability, the typical primate repertoire had expanded and their needs could be made clearer. Now adults could use their tools to break up foodstuffs their children's teeth couldn't manage.

Compared to their predecessors, Habilis infants did need time to learn the extra new ways of staying alive in differing habitats and in hard times. The adult brain would end up bigger as a result of these perceptions, memories and learnt strategies, so from birth onwards it would have to go on growing for longer in order to get there. Infants had their work cut out if they were to be physically competent and socially integrated, and each individual would, of course, have to start from scratch.

~~~~~~~~
~~~~~~~~

As the days went by, a small band of hominins began to make a habit of visiting an area of marsh about half a kilometre along the shore from where the rest of the family had settled, having developed a liking for a kind of nut-grass which grew there. The group usually had in it six females, one with a new-born infant, another with its two year-old female cousin. The leading male, glossy-backed, middle-aged and probably the father of both the youngsters, was followed by two younger males, not yet mature enough to branch off on their own and valuable companions, because their senses were at their sharpest and they had a natural inclination to act as patrols.

For the two year-old, getting along with the males was important. From birth she had always spent more time in the company of her mother and other female relatives, so knew what to expect from them, but she was slightly more wary of the males and their reactions to her approaches were sometimes startling. She recognised each by his face, and by other characteristics – the markedly glossy-back of the leader, the rather tall stature of the one, and the frequent inclination of the other to collect and use stones. But interacting with each of them was dynamic, and put pressure on her social skills.

They had arrived at the marsh and were sitting contentedly chewing on the nut-grass, keeping cool in the shallows at its edge. It was late morning, and the little female, having eaten enough for the moment, was restless, needing the playmates left behind earlier. The tall male was still hot from a chase he'd had warding off a warthog family, and the one nearest to her tickled her for a while but then got bored. She scrambled round to the leader, hoping he'd let her examine his fur for the parasites which lived in it – she ate them, and he was always calm and contented while she probed. The desire to establish herself in his domain was powerful. To her annoyance, however, her aunt had had the same idea, and the glossy-back had already turned round for her to begin. This left him facing the little female, but with eyes closed in anticipation.

Because she had just been eating, the little female's lips were still active. She smacked them together and used her voice to make them loud, driven by her compulsion to distract the glossy-back and induce him to accept her instead.

'bubu..bubu..bubu…!'

It was such an odd noise that the male opened his eyes.

Encouraged, the little female made the noise again. She was certainly getting noticed. She crept closer, and reached out a tentative hand.

'bubu..bubu …' she said as her fingers searched the fur on his arm.

From then on the syllables always made him take notice of her, and that became her normal way of attracting his attention. He would have recognised her by her voice anyway, just as he did every other member of the family – voice conveyed a host of details, like size, gender, mood even - but the odd noise made her stand out, and he came to her aid more readily when she used it. So she benefited in practical ways when situations left her disadvantaged, and in consequence felt a pleasing sense of satisfaction at its effects - something which ensured she would go on including this particular vocal pattern in her repertoire. It was another strand of information to store in the network of details she was accumulating, but differed in that it was something unique to herself[4] – at least for the time being.

The results of many other sensations also had to find room in the little female's brain as the group ranged along the lakeside.

The size of the lake was one thing. Its near shoreline registered, but it took a while to make sense of its horizon. On some days it was a clear, flat line with a grey mass of mountains beyond, but on very misty mornings the mountains vanished, and the distinction between water and sky was blurred. Somewhere in the middle an island rose up, and its prominence, its greenness – the trees and birdlife which could be seen around it – that was easier to handle.

Ever since the days of the Afarensis, hominins had been extending the horizons of their mental as well as their physical lives and understood the lie of many different lands. The plains, rolling hills, mountains, valleys – each had their special characteristics, and the hominins grew up to recognise salient features, inwardly identifying them so that information on each could surface and help direct behaviour as they moved from place to place. With an understanding of the variety of resources and dangers each presented they could cope, and stay alive. The young female learnt quickly about what she saw around her, soaking up new data every day.

Her most forceful impression as she trailed along behind her mother was that without a close opposite bank to swim to, no-one, not even the bold males ventured far from the shore.

She was a ready swimmer though, and where branches overhung streams feeding the lake she and the other youngsters enjoyed themselves by leaping off into the water, repeating and repeating the process until tired or the session was curtailed by the intrusion of other animals.

~~~~~~~~~

As with many young mammals, play was an important occupation for a range of reasons, but in the case of the Habilis, it brought not just physical or social benefits. Games easily became a turn-taking process. It meant being aware of what another individual was doing, and timing the next action. When this was something like landing with a splash the pattern was obvious, but other associated aspects came under its influence too; hearing and copying, listening and responding, answering a call with a call. All were also dependent on having enough control to wait one's turn – and this was a feature that would underpin the way vocal communication developed. It was what a conversation would be like.

Moving in water was also something which demanded control, particularly control of breathing. It needed deeper breaths and a more regulated pattern than most movements, and maybe individuals with a slight genetic advantage would master the art of submerging and surfacing particularly comfortably. They could breathe in, then hold their breath, letting the air out later when they needed to. If that proficiency was shared with other young hominins sired by a leading male, it may not have been all that unusual in Habilis families.

Millions of years before, the Red Sea had flooded down into the Great Rift Valley, creating islands where the land rose higher. Some primate
~~~~~~~~~

populations, finding themselves trapped, could have taken to the water in a desperate bid to escape the consequences of such isolation.[5] Those that managed to turn this misfortune to their advantage learned to swim, and profiting from aquatic food sources, they adapted accordingly. But the long slow millennia led some of them back to a terrestrial lifestyle, and those ancestral hominins who found benefits in walking upright may also have taken some of the legacies of that ancient period with them.

There was the way the covering of body hair aligned itself, and the presence of a thicker layer of subcutaneous fat – a feature which would serve subsequent hominin species very well in the colder times ahead. And then there was the breathing. While moving in water, a greater volume of air would have been needed, so breathing out through the nose just wasn't enough; the mouth had to play a part. Then the windpipe – the larynx – began to move lower down in the throat, occupying a position similar to that found in animals such as seals. This, as far as our own species and eventual spoken language was concerned, was very important indeed, but it would have to wait.

Breath *control*[6] though, was something else; the little Habilis female was already making use of the advantages that a new kind of breath control brought to vocal activities. In a simpler form, being able to start and stop vocalising at will had actually mattered a lot for some time; Afarensis infants might have found that calling could be their life-saver, but if the sound went on for too long it could draw some very unwelcome attention indeed. Inhibiting a call was just as vital as producing it, and young Habilis would surely have arrived with a powerful incentive for cutting short a call when the need arose. Now though, if calls were drawing on whatever was available to enhance them, managing the exhalation of breath *during* a call would be a further valuable refinement.

~~~~~~~~

The attention she'd attracted from the glossy-back had been gratifying, and the little female tried out the string of syllables on the three or four adult members of her group she associated with most closely. But without the original context of urgency the approach hadn't worked. Still experimenting, she took to directing little chains of syllables at some of her youngest kin when they were playing. The patterns might consist of any of the plosive sounds and vowels that lips and tongue could readily combine. However, while the Afarensis had simply merged their sounds into the flow of their calls, with an element of breath control, this young Habilis was finding that a short segment of vocal sounds could be made more interesting, both to herself and to others.

She explored the possibilities. Success appeared to come from making the chain of sounds prominent, like a clump of trees standing tall on the skyline, or the island in the midst of the lake. Habilis brains which had responded to this sort of information to help identify locations might apply the technique again, even if it was being recruited for another purpose. So the little female stressed the chain, and kept it short – just two or three syllables long, and then the others did take notice.

The young of many species make more noise than their elders, and likewise, the infant Habilis
~~~~~~~~

made sounds as they played, and they often played with sounds when they were simply sitting still.[7] They did it on their own, and they did it together and they did it in turns – it was a plaything they didn't get tired of.[8] When they played with the young female, though, it was the leading male's offspring who learnt the two- or three-syllabic sound chains with the greatest ease. They were the older ones, getting to grips with general co-ordination and control anyway – but in them, the breath control came too.

Taking the lead from the young female, they used the chains just as she had done, to identify themselves and each other, gradually developing a system. An individual who often used a particular pattern would respond readily if others copied it back – using it in reply - to attract his attention. Both he and the rest of the family would associate that particular combination with himself, so that it existed alongside his appearance and personal characteristics. The habit didn't take long to spread to those in the wider family who could adapt, and among the rising generations, it was just the thing to prompt helpful reactions to the needs of small hominins. Getting someone's attention quickly could mean the difference between life and death.

It worked the other way round, too. A young hominin, engrossed in searching for grubs in his own patch of vegetation could well be oblivious of threats that were heading his way, but a care-giver, making a sudden alarm call and adding the young one's characteristic sound pattern could be guaranteed a rapid reaction. In a hard world, even quite subtle improvements might enable one family group to thrive where another might fail. All it took was for a higher proportion of adept individuals to survive to maturity so that they could reproduce.

~~~~~~~~~

Whilst it was an advance which may have had its origins in the drawbacks of being small, it didn't have to restrict itself to matters of life and death. When the rising generation did go on to have infants of their own, they would quickly pick up on the fact that the little ones too produced particular chains of sound that could relate to themselves and each other, and it only required care-givers to involve themselves in the turn-taking technique to ensure these labels would stick.

What's more, as it became increasingly purposeful, personal and directed, the new style of vocal activity could have considerable merit later on in life. It could fill a gap.

Travelling imposed stress on Habilis families. Their lifestyle had become one of movement, activated by remembered locations, and even types of location and the drive to benefit from the fruits of their curiosity, but it meant that pauses for physical contact were infrequent. Yet the need for bonding among extended families was stronger than ever. They relied on each other for defence – as a group, especially displaying at a predator, they were effective – and they cooperated with each other in obtaining enough food. More and more they were hungry for animal protein, and more and more the females seemed encumbered by the needs of their infants – they were still learning and needed to stay close - so sharing what they found became essential.
~~~~~~~~~

Mutual grooming or stroking still occurred, but not as often as in earlier times, and because they spread out to forage, the smell of each other was also diluted, carried away on the breeze. Once, keeping in touch had meant exactly that; now a beguiling alternative presented itself. When families came together, more variety in sound-making offered the possibility of a more expressive reflection of the emotions that governed a group's dynamics. What the little female and the generations close to her had tried out grew into 'vocal' grooming. Individuals could even 'groom' on the move.[9]

Early hominin utterances had been mainly emotive – fear, anger, excitement. But in this Habilis family they contained word-like groups of sounds which identified more precisely something that was important to them: each other. Their name-calls (for that was how they operated) could be uttered and replied to – reassurances of proximity, confirmation of who was around by the differences between the calls. Calling and answering was something the birds of the forest did; across the thin early morning sky of the grasslands, skeins of geese made their plaintive contact cries. Now the hominins could do it too, in their own distinctive fashion.

The innovation was clearly a valuable social tool for both infants and adults, but it could have died away with the passing of this generation of inventive hominins. If that had happened the way might have been left open for other options to emerge - maybe gesture would have expanded its repertoire to work well. As the main means of communicating it would have had drawbacks, though, especially for the young, simply because it depended on being seen; if no-one was looking in their direction that was the end of it. An audible system meant everyone heard.

As it proved itself, and went on to establish itself, this was a development influencing relationships, not only within the family but across the wider population, and could have operated at another level – a sexual one; those who vocally enhanced their normal grooming behaviour might well have more mating opportunities than those who didn't.[10] If this was the case, then the tendency towards vocal communication would proliferate with no trouble at all.

<u>The seedbed for spoken language…</u>
- Recognition of prominent features in physical surroundings fed into recognition (and ability to create) prominent features in calls.
- Adaptation to inhibit calls made some breath control possible during vocal activity.
- Use of particular vocal patterns identified familiar individuals.

CHAPTER 4

The Shaping of Tools

Homo habilis (continued)…2 million years ago.

Some adaptations came at a price, however. Quite apart from the neurological mechanisms that hominin brains had developed to power new skills, there was the sheer volume and diversity of information which they were presented with. It was the stuff of life, and there was huge pressure to process it, so their brains continued to grow – and skulls continued to get bigger.[1]

The growth of the brain was, it would seem, both a consequence and a cause of the Habilis capabilities, and was entirely in keeping with the style of other natural expansions. A forest or grassland expanded when wind or rainfall carried small seeds beyond existing boundaries, and so long as suitable climatic conditions prevailed, the process would become self-perpetuating.

So it was with the Habilis. When circumstances drove individuals to their very limits, any advance on what they'd done before would act like a seed carried further, which, in a climate of usefulness, was bound to establish itself. Then, next time hardships were encountered, these new capabilities would provide seed for the next expansion. Slowly and inexorably, surviving was demanding more complex cognitive and technical skills, and all this cleverness was going to their heads.

Which was reasonably fine for those who had adult bodies to carry them round, but what was quite impossible was to have all the valuable wisdom of an adult brain from birth – the skull size would have been much too big. The compromise was for the young to be born at an earlier stage in their neurological development than their predecessors,[2] and although the baby's head would be larger, it was manageable - the female anatomy could cope. Physically a new-born would be a little less coordinated, a little less able to move about, but instinct would kick in and the infant himself would find a way of compensating for his limitations. What he did was to arrive in the world with a furious and persistent urge to get someone else to help when he had needs he couldn't meet on his own.

The solutions which evolved out of this predicament ultimately affected not just Habilis infants and their mothers, but the human species that followed. Because brain size would go on increasing until our own species, homo sapiens emerged. Over hundreds of thousands of years, as the brain grew, infants would have to be born at an earlier and earlier stage of development. So from Habilis onward, the young would be depending on care-givers for longer and longer, and for more wide-ranging kinds of input.

Communication between infants and care-givers would therefore be central to this process – where interactions were effective they maximised an infant's chances: good communicators survived. Crucially, they survived to breed. Although it was obviously only mature individuals who mated, they would be the ones who, as infants, had been quick to understand what they heard and skilful in getting what they needed. It was this that ultimately gave them a selective advantage when it came to reproduction.

So what sort of interactions would have made Habilis infancy such   fertile ground for further growth towards spoken language?

~~~~~~~~

Successive extended family groups had wandered through the Great Rift Valley, inevitably retracing the steps of their ancestors; they were rarely far away   from the lakes that lay strung out over the hundreds of kilometres of its length.

One such group had been living for some time near the largest of these – Lake Turkana – and towards the end of most days its members would make their way steadily towards rising ground, a short way back from its alkaline waters. It was an area of shrubby grassland of the sort that yielded berries at this time of year and at its highest point ended in a rocky escarpment. Perched alone on an outcrop was a young adult female. She was sitting motionless, her face turned towards the last of the day's light. Behind the mountain range the sun had slipped down, spreading its crimson and gold glow across sky and water. With the approach of night, however, had come the first vague tightening in her abdomen, stimuli to move back towards the cover of a dense thicket. It was her first pregnancy, and for some days she had been annoying another female in the group who had given birth four weeks earlier, constantly following and trying to take the baby from her. The other females were alerted by what they saw.

Now she began whimpering, the heavy pressure low down demanding effort to relieve it, and within her tentative alarm calls the young female did as she had often done in situations where company
~~~~~~~~

was needed – play, grooming, attack, defence – she used the name-calls of her close kin. For the Habilis, delivering their young had become a situation where company was needed, because it offered greater safety.

Softly her kin slipped through the shadows, curious and attentive. The young female panted and let out a groan, and around her the other females glanced quickly this way and that, searching the gloom with eyes and ears, fearful that her smell and the noise she made would draw the hyenas. It took a little time, and when the baby came he uttered a feeble cry of his own as the final push released him onto the leaf litter. He lay there a moment, his fur damp and clinging, and immediately his mother reached and pulled him to her, nuzzling and breathing his scent until he latched onto a nipple and was calm.

The hyenas had missed this one, and the females returned to their nests among the bushes, the new mother among them.

As for her son, oblivious of the fine-tuning which had gone into getting him this far, he was going to be dependent for quite a while on the maternal skills of a mother with no previous experience. Certainly, she had observed other females and their young with keen interest, and would have a powerful instinct to promote his survival. But the young of many species have evolved techniques that oblige their parents to feed them – like young wolves nuzzling their mother's mouth, stimulating her to regurgitate food. So it would be the little male who would prompt responses timed to meet his various needs, and up to her to take notice.

In the first few days he remained at her breast, suckling at will and protected by her arm across him. The muscles of his neck weren't quite strong enough to give him complete control of his head and the young female continued supporting him as the days passed and he gained weight. Extreme caution delayed any impulse to put the little male down, and it was only when he himself began to reach for things that caught his interest that she relaxed. For a while he would bleat anxiously if she moved too far away for comfort, because attempts to coordinate his limbs made him slightly unsteady when he wanted to go after her, and the separation was frightening.

To calm him she would direct short calls at him, and while he could hear her voice he didn't cry – he had known it from within the womb.

There was much to be gained by listening to the sound of her voice. She would vocalise, then fall silent as her attention was taken up with foraging; if the little male began whimpering, she would vocalise again. The technique had the effect of reassuring him, but also of training his hearing – teaching him from his earliest days about the tunes and rhythms of her voice,[3] and the subtle shifts in frequency between this or that vowel, and this or that consonant.

Because he stayed close by, he would watch her face too, seeing how her lips moved and her expression changed. It was one of the few things a very young infant could do. He absorbed the way those tunes and rhythms carried the strings of sounds, and how they matched with her obvious contentment or excitement, her fear or her anger.

So when one day after feeding, small tentative sounds escaped the little male's lips, the young female regarded him with interest. She had noticed how he often seemed to be trying to move his tongue and lips as if copying what she did, but this was new.[4] As she listened, there were noises – those his lip and tongue made – which were recognisable, but there were also some gurglings that were altogether different.

The longer period it was taking for the little male to move about on his own had led to him being cradled – often by willing female kin – and in such a position his tongue could loll back. Any crows of satisfaction after a feed were bound to be affected, and what the little male's mother was hearing were sounds like 'g', 'ng' and 'k', produced towards the back of his throat.

Automatically she echoed him, obeying the innate drive for mothers to respond. Her sharp ears had interpreted the acoustics of the unusual noises, directing her tongue so that mimicking was possible, but these sounds wouldn't integrate into her normal repertoire, which were a range of patterns she'd learnt during her own infancy. Fortunately for her offspring however, there were juvenile hominins around who, naturally curious, would also hear the gurglings. For them too it took little effort to imitate what he was doing, but because the activity seemed like a game, it was they who supplied the daily confirmation that the new sounds were interesting and enjoyable. Who but the young would play about with something as apparently pointless as a funny noise – and maybe use it to embellish a vocalisation of their own?[5]

It was how, over many thousands of years, the actions of tongue and lips might slowly add to and establish a multitude of consonants. Enriched in this way, vocal communication would be departing markedly from the ape-like calls out of which it had grown.

After some weeks the little male's ability to get around had improved considerably, but he was still far too unsure of himself to be coaxed into rough and tumble with the juveniles, and he continued to gravitate around the young female. It was she who still served as the primary focus of his vocal activities, being much absorbed with him, and the turn-taking pattern of their contact calls kept both of them feeling secure.

Even when he did venture away, the little male would scramble back whenever he detected urgency in her voice.[6] Any tension she felt raised its pitch, and because this seemed to work, she used it whenever she felt the instinct to keep him near. Vocalisations directed specially at her son were more tuneful, higher than those the young female would use with the rest of her group, and she was rewarded by his obvious swift attention – with outer ear canals still so small, this pitch level resonated perfectly.[7]

For his own part, well after he could walk and climb, if he was hurt or found himself in unfamiliar situations, his cries would bring her hastily to see what was happening. For him it was just the natural urge to get help, another consequence of having been born disadvantaged, but this unconscious strategy would strengthen the young mother's responsiveness, and so provided further reinforcement for vocal communication.

There was however, more to the growing skill than this. The habit of listening and watching had given her son an edge on understanding what was going on around him. Seeking to focus on his mother's face, especially her eyes, had given the little male his first clues to the blurred puzzle of noise, movement, light and colour beyond her arms. When she vocalised, he followed where she looked, and so quite soon he could identify who was who in the family by their name-call, and learnt the way they greeted one another. Well before he was weaned he recognised the foods his mother was eating, the characteristic expressions she used in anticipation of them, and soon too he would be aware of how his family identified the animals with which they shared the landscape.[8]

Mimicking the characteristic sounds each animal made was easy and such 'names' had probably surfaced early in hominin calls, through fear – they were a refinement of the early alarm calls. Knowing what was nearby was vital, and Habilis young were under intense pressure to escape, so motivation to recognise a warning was powerful indeed. Always the little male's attention would fly straight to the speaker's eyes – whoever it was – to tap into what they knew and he didn't.[9] Understanding the differences between the warning calls he heard would be a necessity.

His co-ordination was immature, however, so he wouldn't be able to say these patterns himself until his nervous system was better organised. But he compensated by picking up every clue that was going, and using the best vocal offerings he could manage as a way of expressing himself. His mother continued to be involved in the process, because even before he'd mastered any particular sounds she had responded to whatever effort he made – the expression on his face, the waving of hands or arms – she watched and sensed what his attempts might mean.

On the way to being weaned circumstances arose that forced him to draw on all these resources. The group had left the perimeter of the lake with its unpalatable water - only the few springs and marshes had been of use, and there was now more merit in going beyond the surrounding hills to where the woodland edges met grasslands. This involved an inevitable change of diet. For the little male at his present stage, meat was impossible as were most tubers, and because weaning him was instinctive, at times his mother would move off when he approached, obliging him to seek his own food. It was a difficult period. He could manage to get at grubs and insects and most of the leguminous plants found amongst the grasses, but whenever he tried to reach the branches of berry bushes, as often as not his efforts would land him on the ground. Balance was hard to master, what with bipedalism (which he *wasn't* born with) and a rather large head (which he *was* born with).

He got round this by attempting to recruit anyone nearby. Stretching out his arm in the direction of the berries, he would draw attention by vocalising - attempting the sound patterns he'd heard others use when gathering the fruit. It usually worked, because a sign (and the context) clarified what was as yet indistinct.

It was the needs of an instant which were forging a partnership between innate gestures and emerging vocal communication; his frustrated reaching, rewarded by someone helping him would have reinforced the action, eventually turning it into pointing - and he would then go on doing it on purpose. A simple enough movement, it was probably something else which owed its development to the open environment – what use would pointing be in among the leaves and branches of the forest canopy?

If his vocal efforts were also successful, the small male would begin to use the sounds he made on purpose too. Gestures just happened, as did vocalisations, but making deliberate signs, and moulding his sounds to imitate the patterns he heard around him was enhancing communication, and on this his well-being depended. Even in the long term the link between signing and vocalising would continue to support him - it could always facilitate expression and understanding, whether he was the speaker or the listener.[10]

<center>~~~~~~~~~</center>

Long ago, when variations were beginning to appear in Afarensis calls, it had been coping with new foodstuffs that exercised the muscles responsible. Now, the practice of vocal activity itself was feeding into the way the Habilis coordinated lips, tongue, cheeks and jaws. The muscles themselves, compelled by efforts to move in ways for which they were not designed, got round the problem by growing more fibres and associated nerves and dedicating them to the art of articulation.[11] Fossil evidence cannot, of course, show this directly, but the bones of the Habilis jaw and oral cavity were different from those of the Afarensis, and bear witness to different muscular activity – and that would have included vocal activity.

Habilis infants had arrived armed with the raw material for a tool which had a lot of potential. Using their voices could influence what happened to them in a range of everyday situations – situations which had arisen from lifestyle changes – and to which utterances were bound to adapt. But learning to

70

shape that tool came naturally. Articulating, with all its sensations, *felt* enjoyable and *sounded* interesting, so infants did it for fun and for effect. With maturity came improved coordination, and if older kin used sound combinations more skilfully, making alterations was similarly interesting for the young. So the same process would take place as happened in any other copied activity, like the stripping of twigs, using a stone to crack a nut, and later, flaking a stone. In a vocal community, the model was all around; adults automatically responded to infants, and infants would imitate until their efforts achieved a match; there were always older kin, just a little more proficient, demonstrating how useful vocal communication was.

At every stage during the shaping, individuals would use this tool moment by moment for their own personal ends.[12] Yet ultimately it would become a collective asset, because it was turning into a characteristic of the species as a whole.

Adding yet more factors to communication – transforming gestures into signs, and being able to exert a bit of control on the breath stream – were other aspect of this Habilis achievement. Early vocal communication had been involuntary – a spontaneous reaction to whatever a situation might prompt, but now it was possible to use some of the utterances intentionally. Intelligent animals can be seen to do this too, when they communicate with familiar humans – a dog may bark to be let out, a cat may to mew to be let in.

But these were more than timely calls. They involved a combination of skills demanding some orchestration, and fossil evidence does suggests that changes were taking place inside the skull, and that they related to areas of the brain we associate with language. The left side of the brain was beginning to be dominant.

~~~~~~~~

The small male's family emerged from the woodland along with other local families as they migrated along the edge of the grasslands. The year was coming to a season of even drier weather, and carried with it the promise of additions to their diet. Large passing herds of antelope left the earth littered with seeds from trampled plants, and not only could the hominins pick out the best of these, they could also catch unwary birds too engrossed in feeding for their own good. Out in the open it was also possible to scavenge on the remains of kills from lions and leopards, but with their upright stance the Habilis were visible, so potential victims themselves. To counter this, joining forces with other families in the vicinity had become an advantage rather than just a response to natural rhythms: more company delivered more protection. Together they could hurl stones and rocks at the hyenas and vultures, creating a small, dangerous opportunity.

As they walked, several individuals began searching for stones near where a stream flowed during storms. The water had carried with it debris from the volcanic mountains away to the south, and the Habilis had developed an eye for which type of stone could be relied on to flake so that sharp edges were created.[13]

Among the males was a relative of the young mother. Fully in his prime, he had grown adept at producing scrapers – tools that would remove meat from bones and skin. Experience had taught him
~~~~~~~~

that some localities lacked the hard round pebbles used to strike the chosen stone, and he had brought with him from the lakeside one of these heavy white hammer stones.

His hands were well-used to grasping the implement – holding the chosen core stone in his left hand and the hammer stone in his right. He had thumbs long enough to grasp the stones precisely, and with practice had achieved accuracy in striking the core where he wanted it to break.

The male joined the others when he'd found what he needed, and they settled to shaping the scrapers, watched by several youngsters. They had gathered stones of their own, but would make many attempts before they were rewarded with success.

Further away, and following their own agenda, the females from the various groups made a loose procession, pushing through the thick vegetation by the stream bed for the plants whose roots were still able to get at moisture. They browsed carefully, keeping in contact by calls and signals, always with an eye to the whereabouts of the infants accompanying them. Among them were the young male and his mother. He had walked as much as he could, but the terrain was unforgiving, snagging at him, making him stumble, and he was irritable. The young female lifted him up, lodging him on her hip so that she had a hand free to go on hunting for food. Both he and she would be comfortable like this for quite a while. He habitually nuzzled to her left side, sensing the reassuring regular beat of her heart, so it was to her left hip that she settled him, and it was her right hand that did the work.

Back by the stream bed, the steady percussion of stone on stone faded away as the midday sun intensified its heat, and the males rejoined the females and young in the shade at the edge of the thickets.

They rested until the end of the afternoon, and then began scanning the sky for the vultures. When they appeared, spiralling high on the hot air, the collection of families became alert. With their superb eyesight the birds could detect what was hidden from the Habilis – the whereabouts of the lions or the other big cats and the animals they were chasing. When the bird behaviour changed it was clear that the hunt had succeeded, and the Habilis group approached the kill site – a rough area of grassland. The carcase would be watched from a distance while the scavengers descended upon it, then, when the first frenzy was over, the ablest hominins would drive off whatever was still taking its chance and quickly hack at the carcases with their sharpened tools, dragging the spoils away to the relative safety of trees. Speed was important – hominins were far from top of the pecking order.

The families stayed in the vicinity as long as they dared, scraping flesh from long bones, finally smashing them open to extract the marrowfat. Cats cheated of that particular kill would soon turn their attention elsewhere, seeking new prey. Perhaps that was the fate of the individual whose bones were slowly taken back into the earth at Koobi Fora,[14] east of the long lake.

~~~~~~~~~

Alongside these bones were tools. From the way they were formed, it's clear they were usually made by right-handed individuals. And if females carried
~~~~~~~~~

infants on the left side – the most instinctive choice - by default, the hand most used for gathering and eating food was also the right. This was a form of pressure in both males and females, and the brain, in its evolution, would respond by tending to reflect such concentration of activity in areas on its opposite side – the left prefrontal lobes.[15] But that wasn't all. The whole of the prefrontal cortex was growing, and as vocal communication continued to adjust itself to the needs of its users, connections would be forged within other busy regions of the brain. Stone and voice – both were tools increasing in scope, and the brain would hunger for the energy each demanded.

As time passed, fossil finds and the tools that lay with them suggest that the consumption of meat was intensifying. If our pre-human ancestors made greater efforts to scavenge and hunt, was it changes to their habitat that drove them? If the forests were receding, perhaps meat was what was more widely available – so long as they had the means to obtain it. Or perhaps it was the social behaviours of every day, through which communication entwined itself, which exerted pressure to take new risks. Whatever the causes, the needs of a growing brain itself would be setting the agenda.

<u>The seedbed for spoken language…</u>
- Mother/infant exchanges intensified due to longer and greater dependency.
- Infants gained 'experience' of the wider environment through understanding the communication of others.
- Sound play allowed novel patterns to appear in the repertoire of a close group.
- Infants made greater use of their vocal expression and signs to get needs met.
- Increasing reliance on vocal communication would demand specialisation of the brain, as it reflected needs which altered as the individual matured.
- By adulthood, other behaviours such as stone tool-making and carrying infants contributed to lateralisation in an enlarging brain – evidence of specialisation in an area of the brain also involved with language.

CHAPTER 5

Family Influence

Homo ergaster...1.8 million years ago.

To the south-east of Lake Turkana was an immense funnel-shaped depression. It lay between the high plateau to the north and mountain ranges to the south. When the climate allowed, a major river flowed through from the lake to the distant sea,[1] accompanied by its vegetation and associated wildlife. There were also, however, wide areas of mixed bush land, and as the years had passed in their thousands and in their tens of thousands, instead of the heavy rainfall that had once fed steamy forests, a hot sun baked the ground. Across the changeable mosaic of the landscape, the bush and grasslands were beginning to dominate.

As the tropical forests shrank, the inhabitants of this swathe of the African continent did as always – whatever was possible under the circumstances. Some of these inhabitants were other hominin species, and inevitably they would have displayed some features of physique and behaviour in common with the Habilis. What they all shared though was an uncertain future, a future that has faded into an uncharted past, because the fossil record is sparse and can be contradictory. So it's hard to discern whether there was a direct connection between the Habilis and the next most likely ancestor to ourselves – *Homo ergaster,* (sometimes described as African *Homo erectus*).

Whoever their predecessors were, though, *Homo ergaster* arrived on the scene with the potential for greater enhancement of vocal communication and an increasing ability to make stone tools – we know this because there's evidence in Ergaster remains for both these skills. Perhaps most relevant of all was a continuing flexibility of approach to the demands of survival. *Homo ergaster*, the first hominin to cross the threshold into being human, would demonstrate this during the following 600,000 years, thanks to a brain that was continuing to get bigger. It was organising itself in response to new challenges - so among these what was it having to tackle that caused vocal communication to grow into the beginnings of spoken language?

Inevitably, these hominins would be confronted by years when the weather reverted to patterns of extreme wet alternating with blistering heat, and their populations might dwindle through misfortune or adaptations that, in the end, didn't quite work. But on the whole it was the dry trend which was establishing itself, and their neural, physical and behavioural adjustments were being tempered accordingly.

Homo ergaster families would have been obliged to find more ways of getting by out on the plains. It was a risky business; away from the trees they were on a par with any other grassland animal, presenting as prey to be stalked and hunted down by carnivores adapted for the purpose. But they were eating more meat, so that risk was being managed – not just with the weapons they were using, but also in the way they understood their environment.

And eventually, fossils of *Homo ergaster* would be discovered far, far away, in Asia. Step by step they had walked into the unknown.   If these ancestral humans could explore like this, with the confidence to trust their curiosity, something beyond animal cunning and luck must have been at work. Inside the brain cognitive skills were allowing the Ergaster to assess the landscapes before them and make places for themselves and their families. Memory was involved, perceptiveness was involved, social issues were involved – and vocal communication was involved, growing and developing out of whatever had gone before.

~~~~~~~~

Over some months a small colony of family groups had been making its way south-eastwards across what, in years past, had been the Turkana River basin. The Afarensis and Habilis had been similar in height, but Ergaster hominins had been growing taller as the millennia wore on. Even so, faced with new terrains they used higher ground wherever they could, wanting the view it gave them over the bush lands.

A forward party, reaching the summit of rising ground well ahead of the rest, suddenly drew to a halt. They had been following tracks and signs for some while and now, in the late afternoon, the effort involved had raised a sweat.[2] It was something the body had managed as a way of cooling the skin, and it had further widened the distinction between hominins and the primates who inhabited the forests. Thick coats of fur had grown sparse over much of the body, and against the rays of the sun the skin was developing other protection, colouring itself brown. Up here though there was neither camouflage nor cover for them, and the scouts
~~~~~~~~

dropped to a crouch, approaching the edge of the escarpment with care.

The question of finding water was of constant, practical concern.[3] If it could be derived from what the Ergaster ate the problem was less acute, but sometimes during the years when large parts of the land were cooler and parched, the Ergaster needed to take their cue from the wildlife around them. Elephants had been contributors to hominin success since before the forests retreated, gathering their own vast quantities of food and trampling corridors through the dense jungles to the clearings they had created around freshwater springs. They grew old and could remember the routes, even now, across the changing landscape. They were reliable guides and their knowledge could be borrowed.

In the distance, and despite the haze, the scouts could see the elephants they had been following. They watched as the huge animals drank and wallowed, spraying themselves at a circular waterhole. This was what they'd been seeking, but with the coming of dusk, getting at the precious water would be too hazardous and the Ergaster families would have to wait for dawn to take their chance.

The forward party turned back to the place where the rest of the families had settled – grubbing for anything edible in the scrub surrounding a copse of trees. Those who had stayed behind were a mixed group composed of some reasonably able elders, juveniles, and of course, the young with their mothers. Even here in amongst the trees, the latter no longer instantly took to the branches when apprehensive - anatomical changes in females and heavier infants saw to that.[4] Trees were still climbed, though – for the food available – because youngsters played in them and kept the ability going, but the canopy wasn't home any more.

There were other problems, too; young Ergaster would have clutched in vain for the thick coats of fur which their forest predecessors had clung to, when mothers and other kin were ready transport, simply by passing near enough to be grabbed. Now it was up to the little ones themselves to hail their care-givers, and instead of hauling themselves on board, they had to persuade someone to pick them up and carry them.

Persuasion was not a problem. Firstly they had voices disproportionately loud for their size;[5] secondly their sounds had evolved so that the pitch was just right for cutting through the incessant clamour of insects and birds, or the shifting wind, or the crisp rustle of dry grass;[6] and thirdly, a commotion like that could create a dangerous situation or make another even more perilous. No-one ignored them.

Not that such family groups were defenceless. By a concerted effort of well-aimed missiles and vigorous, aggressive displays, they could look after themselves under many circumstances. What they couldn't do for themselves, however, was travel at speed and know what lay ahead and out of sight.

To fill this gap they relied on others - individuals whose experience over time had taught them how to distinguish one tract of land that could support the families from another that wouldn't, and could sense which direction they should go. Wandering aimlessly was not an option.

So in among the trees, those waiting were on the look-out for the returning scouts, listening and watching intently. The first scouts came through the scrub and the sound of their voices carried the message they wanted to hear. Prominent in the calling were highly stressed, repeated features:

"Ayleeya…….ahkooah!"

By these syllables, the excitement in their voices, and the positive demeanour, the families now did know. The elephants were there; water was there.

~~~~~~~~~

Sound patterns - words - could acquire a new and very powerful attribute. Whereas before, hominin word-like utterances could behave like labels, identifying what or who could be seen or heard at that same moment, now they could stand in to represent the real thing when it *couldn't* be seen – a particular combination of sounds understood as though it was indeed the real thing. This was a significant development: vocal communication was becoming symbolic.

It was an innovation certainly, but for a well-organised brain, not an unlikely one. The Ergaster ability to memorise had been honed long ago by the necessity of dealing with the seasonal availability of food, and the locations of particular items. So even if a fruit were plucked from its bush and carried back, other individuals seeing it would be reminded – visual messages would be sent winging around the brain from cell to cell, area to area. Its appearance would act as a trigger to a range of responses – knowing what kind of fruit it was told them which bush to go looking for, and where it grew. Now these hominins were exploring more extensively, and new foods were being discovered.
~~~~~~~~~

The pressure would be on for ways of making it easier to remember information about them.

A specific sound pattern – a word – could do that: it tapped into the same system. Plucked from its original context (uttered when a food item was noticed) the word said later could stand in for the real thing – not a visual message, but an auditory one, just as capable of winging around to gather information gleaned from past experience, and just as capable of prompting a response.

<div align="center">~~~~~~~~</div>

In the morning the information would indeed be acted upon. After the elephants had had their fill at the waterhole, so would the Ergaster.

As the days passed, those who could do so banded together to ambush any small or weak animals which might lag behind en route to drink, and the reedy margins were scoured for their harvest. The urgent drive for water had receded, and the families blended the rhythm of their lives to that of the comings and goings at the waterhole, occupying any surrounding areas of vegetation capable of providing cover

It was a fine situation for adults who could make their own way to satisfy thirst. But needing to drink more often, how would an infant fare? Even if reasonably bipedal, going out there alone was hazardous.   For the young, ever watchful and attentive to what took place within the group, the effect and implications of the sound pattern 'ahkooah' could readily be absorbed. As soon as they could copy what they heard, there was the solution. Say 'ahkooah', say it often, (say it loud) and a nearby adult would take you to drink.   It worked whether or not the water was in sight; and success in using this symbolic pattern of sounds made the process 'click', so that infants would tend to add other words to their vocabulary.

By managing to coordinate lips, tongue, voice and breath, infant hominins improved their lot no end. They could make it clear when they wanted something, or if parts of the body got hurt during play. Gradually they would learn that any aspect of Ergaster life might be represented by a word, but it would be a collection of sounds that related to the whole experience. Words heard and uttered were part of the experience itself.[7]

But if vocal proficiency was showing its worth in practical terms, the way spoken language might ultimately emerge was also being influenced, albeit indirectly, by a shift in how Ergaster society was having to function.

In one of the shadier wooded areas, one of the family groups had settled in amongst the palms, scouring the ground for nuts and fallen fruit. These supplies were coming to an end, and females with young relied more and more on returning males for what they were bringing back. A degree of food-sharing had taken place for a long time in accordance with traditional hierarchies of dominance, whether between males, females or across genders and ages. Now, though, something different was happening.

This family included a female with both a new-born infant and a four year-old. The latter was physically competent, but still remained close to her mother and the other females, learning by listening, watching and experimenting how to deal with the demands of daily life. The obligation this imposed on her mother – to go at the speed of her offspring

– was repeated to a greater or lesser degree for all of the females with young, so they tended to associate closely, mindful of the whereabouts of each other and their active infants.

It also tended to perpetuate a widening division in feeding habits, with females largely foraging, and males engaging from time to time in the more dangerous and lengthy expeditions to gain meat, less accessible fruits, and occasionally, honey. In the distant past, the offspring of earlier ancestral species would have been mobile within a matter of weeks, and so separate individuals, but now the two had to remain close for many months. So the males, mindful of which females they had impregnated, might return more exclusively to them, and continue to do so even after the infants were born. By providing extra fats and sugars for the mothers while they were most restricted, the males made doubly sure of their own genetic survival. For their part, the females usually responded with something from their day's pickings.[8]

Under the palm trees the four year-old was keeping an eye out for her mother's mate to return. She was more familiar with him than with the other males – the sound of his voice, and the way he moved when the groups were all together. He had returned to mate with her mother this time largely due to the bond formed during the period he had shared food while she herself was new-born.

~~~~~~~

This was a trend in social organisation which was going to persist for a very good reason. Females were becoming larger in relation to males, thanks
~~~~~~~

to being better nourished. And during the later stages of pregnancy meat would have been hard to come by if they'd had to obtain it themselves. But for the males, bringing food back was worth the extra effort: their offspring were healthier so more would survive, and as far as the future of the species was concerned, more would go on to breed.

Coincidentally, a stable or increasing population, living in relatively close proximity, provided ideal conditions for emerging vocal skills to proliferate and go on developing, whether they related to practical, personal or social matters. Ergaster hominins would be using their enhanced version of primate vocal communication throughout their adult lives, automatically, whenever situations prompted it, and it was available to them because they'd grown up with it. What maintained and stimulated the skill were the interactions they experienced with a range of generations every single day. It was how their first simple, instinctive vocalisations gradually moulded themselves into progressively more meaningful utterances, understood by the wider community.

As in any species, where specific variations in calls are understood by its members – aggression, warnings, mating readiness and so forth - so it was with the Ergaster. For them, whenever new layers of meaning were added, inside the heads of all the individual members of families was a mutual interpretation – particular utterances meant the same to everyone. So a flourishing peer group, young siblings, older cousins, kin in general – around and available at every stage - all played a necessary part in nurturing and promoting the skill in the young, although as in any animal, the process was not a conscious one.

Given that there were distinctions between male and female lifestyles in Ergaster society, maybe even at this early stage there were also subtle consequences for spoken language in terms of gender differences. When females foraged their low-profile contact calling with young and each other would have been an important element in their sense of security. Vocal activity was integrated into the things they did. For young males it may not have been quite the same though; once they were sufficiently adept physically, their interest inevitably turned towards accompanying older males and forming their own cohorts, and they would leave the females. They had other priorities. They needed to observe and imitate action and often keeping quiet helped concentration – and was safer. Vocal communication could function slightly differently for them, and maybe this was a faint hint that eventually spoken language would tend to bloom more readily in infant females than in infant males.[9]

~~~~~~~~

The small female was already chattering to herself with anticipation, but before she could let her mother's mate know she was there watching for him, an old male acting as a guard at the edge of the woods had already begun the greeting ritual as he came into view. With rising tones he used the name-call associated with this particular individual. Her own excited call, though, was different.

"Papa...papa...papa...!"

It was the simple repeated syllable, common amongst many young Ergaster which had grown
~~~~~~~~

out of early sounds mumbled against their mother's breast, and reinforced in the usual way – it attracted interest. Weaning wasn't really complete until sometime in the third year, so when her father appeared with food, she'd ceased suckling, focusing her eyes on his face. He'd noticed her gaze, returning it, and as her lips sought out the nipple again, his automatic response to her soft sounds was to answer – to copy, "*papapa*", and to stroke her face with his finger.

~~~~~~~~

Ergaster babies, like the new-born of the earlier species, had of course precious few ways of attracting (and maintaining) interest, given their physical limitations. If the next meal didn't appear, that was it. They'd instinctively used their voices as one sure way of getting noticed, and not long afterwards maybe another useful strategy presented itself. They could often be left in the care of other females, but the separation might go on too long for comfort. Then, anxiety or hunger always showed on their faces: lips were drawn back with tension, turning into excitement as mothers came close with milk and reassurance. It was a facial expression – a 'low closed grin' - which the Ergaster shared with the chimpanzees, but maybe they adapted it a little to their advantage. As the days passed, babies gained in confidence, and the tension turned into a more positive sensation at the sight of their mothers - a facial expression that was also a kind of reward. Mothers themselves needed encouragement to go on caring for their helpless young, and this small sign was an inducement - something along the lines of the extravagant gape
~~~~~~~~

of newly hatched nestlings, but considerably more beguiling. Attention was maintained – and the valuable habit prolonged right into adulthood, as a smile.[10]

~~~~~~~~

So the two hominins now showed their pleasure at seeing each other with smiles. Then the male leaned down to her as she gambolled towards him, pouting his lips towards hers. She had caught a large grasshopper while waiting, and, eager to retain his interest, held it up, saying its name – a series of clicks and rasps similar to the insect's own calls, made by sudden contractions and frictions at the back of her tongue.

"*Ki - hhee, papa, ki - hhee....*"

He looked then, and said it too, and she could see from his eyes that he was pleased. Automatically he reached to accept the grasshopper, but a faint shadow of disappointment on her face changed his mind, and he straightened, letting her know the creature was hers to eat. There had been value in the longer, closer relationship they had – each could pick up on the briefest of cues displaying mood or intention, and such understanding fostered the necessary cooperation within a society growing increasingly interdependent.[11] And it was this change in family structure which allowed spoken language to develop, because underneath, it too needed cooperation between speaker and listener, a system of give-and-take – someone to listen while another spoke.

The two joined the female and her infant. More greetings were exchanged, a tactile, sensory
~~~~~~~~

manoeuvre, accompanied by quiet vocal routines. The male was already absorbing the smell of his latest offspring, a son, and it would sink deep into his awareness of him. They shared in the food he'd brought, then sat digesting it – an easier and shorter process in these hominins than in their predecessors, since the digestive system had obligingly evolved to cope more efficiently.[12] Better quality protein and the fat from meat were the fast food a hungry brain demanded.

The small female, still eager for contact with the male now stretched out on her back, and began a cajoling chatter in which the syllable "*tik*" appeared with increasing frequency. She was pointing to his hand, and then glancing up at his face. He responded by turning and tickling her, just as she had wanted. He'd known what she meant, of course – "*tik*" identified finger, or hand, and in this context could obviously do very well to mean tickle. These syllables might have started off simply enough, but new contexts were always arising that needed understanding; if a syllable's relevance could be stretched to do a slightly different job, then that's what it did. And as in this instance, some utterances were stretching to name activities, as well as parts of the body (including those involved in bodily functions), individuals, animals and food.[13] Chimpanzees might have had the potential to understand such things, but it was the hominins' articulatory skills which had opened the way for that understanding to be expressed in an audible form.

But the food he'd brought was barely enough to satisfy the three of them. The waterhole was shrinking, and all the animals using it were edgy and easily unnerved. The Ergaster males couldn't afford to attract aggression towards their families by causing further commotion, so they resorted to searching among the rocks and bushes further along the escarpment, where they could see what was coming - or rather, as in this instance, going.

A small troop of baboons had been moving off after feeding there and the Ergaster males approached with such stealth that the baboons were unaware of their presence. As they darted among the rocks, two or three stragglers offered opportunity, and these were swiftly taken, but the kill sent the rest of the troop screaming and scattering along the ridge. It was a small bounty, but carried back to share, and pieces were duly relinquished according to the status of the hunters. The meat was a welcome addition to the berries, grubs and insects collected by the females.

Tongues were having to get round food of many kinds now, and all the muscles involved in biting and manoeuvring, chewing and swallowing were lending their agility to acts of speaking. As the ingredients of the Ergaster diet accumulated, so did the ingredients of their sound repertoire.

When night fell, all the family groups who had foraged in the neighbouring countryside drew together, congregating for comfort and safety. They could be reasonably secure like this, in spite of the darkness. Armed by the habit of amassing caches of stones, bones and sticks they could ward off prowling nocturnal animals. Later there would always be individuals who slept lightly enough to raise the alarm. When gathering like this, and before settling down, they would take some of the sticks to use as of old, to beat against tree trunks or the ground, unifying the groups and at the same time asserting their presence.

The Ergaster of course existed as participants in the earth's most fundamental cycles, but individually, each small pulse also had its own vital rhythm. So drumming came from way down, a collective reassurance whenever they made it and heard it, feeling it reverberate through every fibre. Rocking and swaying, or pacing the ground, their voices surged up, inseparable from the mood and the movement.[14]

This inner rhythm permeated the process by which spoken language was beginning to form too. When they uttered the meaningful sound-chains – words – whether in isolation or as elements in general calls, there was an ebb and flow which shaped cadences, just as of old, when the forest throbbed and they'd made their voices heard there. In the brain, it was the right side that carried on dealing with the music – the voice rising and falling on its tides of emotions – so that   the tunes of spoken language tapped into the very deepest and most ancient well of communication.[15] Words had begun coming along later, when the left side of the brain was busy tackling the control and ordering of movements, with special emphasis on the right hand: how to flake a stone, how to gather the food to live while calming an infant against the heart. Being part of the scene, the words had sidled along as well, and slowly began adding their own powerful influence.[16]

Finally the tumult subsided, but the hominins had been calling back and forth for longer than usual, and the pace of the beating sticks had been quickened, fuelled by anxiety. The Ergaster were disturbed by increasing hunger and the situation at the waterhole. The agitation was familiar, however, and a precursor of what would take place the next day.

As dawn broke, the Ergaster took what moisture they could. The dry ground still supported some large-leaved plants where the original edge of the waterhole had been, and the cool night air had caused condensation to collect in the hollow at the base of the stems. After drinking, the families moved off, following the leading males as they had done many weeks before and many times before.

The bank of knowledge carried inside their heads meant that even if the lie of the land was new to them, the mosaic of vegetation which covered it would probably be of types they understood. They could assess the likely value of what they saw. And when they were unsure, the careful curiosity which had often paid off in the past might do so again.

Among the groups, the little family of male, female, new-born and infant advanced as had become their usual practice. In the heat of the day they would stop to rest, then the female would glean from the bushes and grassland, keeping contact with her particular group, through the vocal calls which applied to what was edible and who was nearby, and maintaining links with her mobile youngster. It was only this watchfulness that made it possible for the little female to amass her own bank of knowledge. Often the whole group would fall silent, intent on listening, all watching a particular clump of grass where one had seen movement; then the habit of sharing attention was as much a safety issue as of working out what hid there. But it had other applications. On any occasion when an infant seemed engrossed in looking at something, observant companions automatically followed his or her gaze, identifying the object of interest and building up understanding by using the sounds, signs and gestures associated with whatever it happened to be.[17] The cubs of many of the large carnivores stayed with their mothers until they had learned the skills of hunting; the Ergaster infants were going one better.

For his part, the adult male of the young family would range further afield as one of a number of small bands, seeking the signs of small prey and the predators whose kills might be exploited – perhaps not today, but while they moved within the territory. For much of the time, each band would rely on silence for its effectiveness. Signals and facial expression conveyed what was required during the activity, but once the forays came to an end, voices could give vent to frustration or anticipation, with specific patterns within their calls which would confirm animals seen or suspected. There were gestures and signals which might also help to indicate the direction or landmark feature they'd need to see if they were to return another time.

Not that any of this was a consciously selected technique; the brain processed information and action was the consequence. Many movements of hand and arm were no more deliberate than the muscular contractions that caused a face to convey surprise, fear or contentment. But as hominins matured, the gestures and verbalising – the use of patterns of sounds specifically applied – were becoming more focused. They were both also capable of inhibition – and that meant control. Previously every response had been as automatic as the leopard's explosive speed, or sudden upright tail. And although the Ergaster were still only small-time hunters compared to the swift and lethal cats, because they were communicating like this, they were getting much more adept at scavenging from them.

Occasionally, some of the males would be away for a couple of days or more, and the groups would wait till all were assembled again before continuing their trek.

It had by now been a long time since rain had fallen. When the wind raced across the parched grassland, dust clouds brought the groups to a halt, turning their backs to crouch with hands covering their faces. Conditions such as these made progress slow, and even afterwards, when they resumed their steady stride, the discomfort of such dry air in throats and lungs affected how well they could travel.

The little family with its small infants somehow did better than others; the new-born was still light enough to be carried at the breast, so not a problem, but the reason they managed to keep going may have been the slight advantage possessed by all four – a rather prominent nose. Whereas Habilis faces had been typically flat and sloping, within some Ergaster populations the face was becoming more rounded. And what a larger nose did was to bestow on its owner a facility for moistening the air as it was breathed – and that really helped.[18]

The group had been walking side-on to the wind. It was increasingly important for them to reach the forested slopes of the hills which lay to the south, and with visibility reduced by the dust storm, what they relied on was detecting the scent of the trees. Those who noticed it – individuals with a sense of smell least impeded by dust – turned in response, and their change of direction prompted other groups to follow.

When they reached the forest it would provide resources familiar to them, and the Ergaster families might work their way along the foothills, perhaps eventually turning back the way they'd come. But some also looked ahead, interpreting what the wildlife and vegetation told them, and they too managed to keep going, finding new landscapes and new opportunities.

~~~~~~~~

They were surviving thanks to a combination of features – physical adaptations to the climate, social changes which increased the health of females and infants, and cognitive developments which enabled them to deal with new environments: sensory input into the brain was being perceived, organised, and retrieved in ways that moved them away from their predecessors and towards ourselves. None of these developments would have by-passed communication, and if something approaching verbal expression and comprehension was integral to daily life, those who used it to their best advantage would be those who succeeded. They would survive infancy, function socially, rear offspring – and pass on to subsequent generations those features which, among other things, underpinned spoken language.[19]

Homo ergaster growth patterns were not far different from our own; their children took time to reach maturity, although they had a much shorter adolescence and had probably finished growing by the age of about 12. But whatever else the Ergaster were doing, there's no escaping the conclusion that
~~~~~~~~

they had to continue care-giving long enough for infants to acquire the range of life skills they needed. Compared to older relatives, youngsters were at a disadvantage long-term. But in infancy the neural system was brilliantly pliant, and while infants couldn't do much about being small, weak or inexperienced, in the social set-up of *Homo ergaster* they could exploit communication both in the short term and in the long term. Getting to grips with situations that Ergaster families encountered was quite enough to prompt more developments.

The seedbed for spoken language...
- Specific sound patterns (words) could take on a symbolic role.
- Social changes provided the ideal conditions for verbal language to grow - interplay between close family members.
- Sharing attention within close groups encouraged infants to learn from their elders.
- More personal cooperative behaviour paved the way for the cooperation needed for spoken language to work.
- Communal singing reinforced the rhythmic nature of spoken language.

CHAPTER 6

A Word or Two

Homo ergaster (continued)…1.7 million years ago.

Ergaster hominins had still continued to inhabit, explore and exploit the region once watered by the Turkana River, but for a long while its ancient course had been marked by nothing more than a litter of tiny island mounds, each with its thin, contorted tree, isolated bizarrely in a bed of dark red sand. Then, suddenly the thing had awoken. The river reclaimed its territory, bursting over the dry banks in a show of ferocity, then subsiding to send waves of muddy water hurtling through the valley. Now, only days later, it was meandering serenely through a plain ablaze with flowers.

The storms preceding this phenomenon had been horrendous – black lowering clouds, lightning tearing through the sky, and thunder bombarding the landscape as though to shake it apart.

From their position at the edge of woodland, a cluster of Ergaster families had watched the process with alternating fear and instinctive curiosity. Year after year deciduous leaves had crackled and powdered underfoot, and the grassland with its scattering of flat-topped acacias had stretched into the distance, shimmering under a pale sky. Now the familiar landscape was transformed, and it initially generated huge uncertainty. Mixed in with this emotion however, was a heightened awareness that the difference might also be of benefit. Through every sense they had, the Ergaster were weighing up the scenes before them.

Aromas rose up from the damp vegetation, penetrating deep into the memory, searching its fund of experience. Facial expression, posture and movement revealed feelings, but what their voices carried was the audible outcome of activity in the brain. Sounds and syllables flurried back and forth, and for older individuals it was a miniature storm of recollections which sparked and converged, flashing an instant message to the muscle fibres of voice and gesture, conveying something over and above an involuntary reaction to the drama. Even if individual banks of knowledge were incomplete, their vocalising allowed a pooling of information, and it began raising their confidence to investigate whatever the turbulent weather had thrown their way. So for a day or two they lingered close to the woods, periodically breaking into lengthy calls, in which the names for foodstuffs, prey animals and predators were interwoven, until they had identified possibilities and felt prepared enough to risk taking a look.

Now the string of families was edging warily down towards the river. The new green of the vegetation offered the promise of a succulent meal. What restrained them, however, was also carried on the air:

"*Heepoh, cokoda!*"

The words were barked, softly, urgently, by the oldest individual among the families. He kept repeating them. Long before, during a spell of tropical storms similar to these, he'd encountered too closely the inhabitants of a swollen river and its damp reed beds. Thereafter, whenever he'd caught sight of hippos or crocodiles near waterholes, he'd been the first to utter the sound patterns associated with them. Those closest to him echoed the words, and a ripple of repetition spread through the approaching groups, but it was automatic, and for younger individuals, inevitably without real understanding. The old male's fear came from knowing at first hand just how dangerous the animals could be. Perhaps resident in some isolated area of marshland, at the onset of the storm they had sought out the river. Now, like the Ergaster, they were eager for food.

His agitation increased as, attracted by the profusion of new foodstuff, individuals and little groups of hominins began splitting off, plucking shoots out of the damp meadow and settling comfortably on the moist ground to taste and savour what they'd found. He called again, more loudly, and this time his warning was heeded; all the hominins stood up, taking note of the smooth grey mounds in the centre of the muddy river, and, when he pointed, they saw the row of long serrated backs lying motionless where the river widened and became shallow.

One of the groups included a family of male, female and two infants. At seven years old, the young female would always look out for her three year-old brother. In the present unusual situation, though, all young hominins and their mothers sought each other out, and together they gravitated towards the males who had provided food and protection earlier in their lives. Physically the difference in size between male and female hominins had stabilised, and there would be no further change in proportions in the species that followed. Looking after females, it seemed, had worked better than competing for them and being big had lost its advantage.[1] The large brain was proving the greater asset, and now it would go on doing so.

The old male scanned the reforming groups, watched till they had resumed feeding, then grunted and set to satisfying his own hunger.

After a while, when all seemed calm, the two youngsters began trying to get a better look at the river. They'd been hungry, but were satisfied more quickly than their elders and they slipped away as the adults became more engrossed in probing through the vegetation.

The sinuous writhing of the brown water was fascinating. Branches of trees, carried along on the current spun and sank, then reappeared to claw at the air. Along the edge, waves licked at the earth, sometimes devouring chunks of it, so that in places the bank overhung the river. And then there were the hippos, visible some distance downstream, wallowing in a broad bend of slow-moving water. The young Ergaster took it all in, focused completely on these unfamiliar sights.

They continued to follow its course upstream, until they found a place where it was just possible to get down. Being older and bolder, the young female clambered down, leaving her brother on the bank. He watched, ready to go as well, and then saw her stop suddenly as something launched itself into the river.

He made the connection with the old male's emphatic call: "*Cokoda, cokoda!!*"

The young female could just see the crocodile and she too registered the name, but it was the sight of the creature's movement through the water that kept her transfixed.

From his vantage point above, her brother's attention switched to several similar shapes on a strip of mud further away, on the opposite side and out of sight from the female because of the height of the bank.

"*Cokoda*" he shouted, and again, his voice rising, "*Cokoda!!*" He was frantic now, seeing that all the beasts were stirring.

The young female had started retreating from the edge of the water, but not nearly fast enough.

"*Cokoda!!*" He tried again, pointing towards them. It dawned on him that she couldn't see them. He was incapable of physically coming to her aid, but under stress, other options tore through his mind, and a word burst from his lips that he'd used to his sister many times:

"*Moh… moh!*"

Then the two impulses fused.

"*Moh cokoda….. moh!*" Then at the top of his voice, "*moh cokoda, moh cokoda, moh cokoda!*"

Then the young female did react, with a leap of understanding that this crocodile wasn't the only one. "*Moh*" was what her brother said when he wanted more food – more of the berries she had in her hand. He meant *More crocodiles*!

She hurled herself at the bank, grabbing at reeds and tufts of grass. Behind her, the first crocodile was emerging from the river. She had slid down there easily enough; getting back up took all her strength. The young male was screaming with terror, and the grass was coming away in her hands.

The family groups had heard the young male's first call. The parents had instantly stood up, answering him, and everyone reacted to the sudden disturbance. Recognising the alarm in the voices and the fearful word, they began rushing to the river, picking up anything they could hurl or use to beat the reptiles off. It was almost too late.

With its jaws widening the creature was within striking distance of the female's scrabbling feet when sticks and clods of earth caught the side of its head, checking its speed. The adults reached for her hands and pulled, dragging her onto the bank. She lay there, trembling, panting and wailing, but was hauled upright so that they could all get away from the hideous long heads and fury of lashing tails.

It took some time for the family to settle back into foraging, and night found all the groups well back from the river, positioned on rising ground where they might be forewarned of anything approaching. In the brief period of dusk, sitting close to their mother, the young Ergaster repeated over and over the words that related to what had happened to them.

"*Cokoda, cokoda, moh cokoda…*"

Sometimes it became like a chorus, with both voices expressing the overwhelming fear they'd felt. The valuable instinct to escape would be strengthened by what had happened, but with the added ingredient of words there was a downside. Without words, an unpleasant memory could fade and the fear would only be revived by reality. Captured in a word, however, recorded as a sound pattern in the brain, the experience could come back any time, revived inside the brain; the fear might never go away.[2]

For now, though, the reliving of it all somehow reduced the intensity of emotion, because the situation wasn't quite the same; here they were safely surrounded by kinsfolk, well away from the cause of their fear. Using the words did help deal with it, confirming that the danger was over.

~~~~~~~~

Perhaps the most telling feature of the utterance, however, was the single syllable used by the little male in a way that created a crucial link between two bits of information - the sounds meaning 'more'. Such a syllable had started out vaguely enough – a mumble that slipped from his and other infants' lips when feeding. Not satisfied, they reinforced the simple utterance with a reaching hand and often as not managed to beg another morsel. The same vague sound could prompt someone to go on playing a game, or go on grooming. It was a general purpose syllable that normally worked perfectly well on its own.

What was significant in this instance, therefore, was that the one utterance - *"moh"*- had been able to add something to the meaning of another. Hominin vocalisations were moving yet further away from the kind of calls that other animals made. *Visible* information, such as posture, gesture and facial expression underpinned any act of communication, certainly, but increased precision of meaning, conveyed audibly, owed its emergence to this sort of growth. The Ergaster brain had, after all, been responsible for the process of simple tool-making – a task which itself required two stones to be brought together so that one might have an effect on the other. If it could do it with stones it could probably do it with words.

There was another aspect of vocal communication that was coming to the fore, too:
~~~~~~~~

nothing in the actual sound of "*moh*" hinted at its meaning.

For hundreds of thousands of years the practice of converting something seen and heard into something vocally expressed had probably drawn on the brain's own perceptions.[3] For instance, a possible early word for the heron whose nests the Ergaster raided - "*cak-cak-cak*", could have been an imitation of the birds' distinctive call, just as we identify some birds today - chiff-chaffs, for example, or hoopoe. The sound heard primes the brain to draw out of the vocal system an utterance following the same familiar acoustic contours. In a similar way, other characteristics, including physical ones, could be represented – a hole (somewhere a small prey animal might be found, or even a cave or rock shelter for the Ergaster themselves to use) could be "*kolo*": the visual impulses which registered its roundness on the receptive brain, turned about and became the outcome – rounded lips making a rounded sound. Even today, experiments show that people recognise a quality in the sound of some words which hints at their meanings. In its earliest forms 'naming' was self-generated information, and so closely connected to whatever had prompted it that it could be processed instantly – the word couldn't be separated from its meaning.

"*Moh*", however, was different. It didn't have a shape to mimic or a sound to copy. It might have come randomly, but had then caught on from being so often used in particular contexts. The meaning of the syllable was understood because the situations themselves were understood.

In much the same way, signals routinely made with hands and arms conveying direction ('up','down') or location ('here', 'there') might habitually be accompanied by a specific vocalisation, as would body movements expressing assent or dissent and possession – more words in the making.

And given that the evidence for Ergaster advances in tool-making and tool use reflect adult capabilities, it would be tempting to think that such verbal refinements would also be the province of adults. But it would still have been infants who were the driving force. It was they who were hardest hit by the everyday impacts of getting to grips with learning to walk and getting along in their social group. So those who enhanced their calls for help – to scramble *up* rocky outcrops, to get *down* from the branches of a tree, to claim a fruit as *mine* – may have managed marginally better than those who didn't. Words would persist as an essential feature of adult communication, because uncertainty, fearfulness and possessiveness didn't just melt away with advancing years. Verbal expression, understanding and remembering could generate a sense that situations might in some way be grasped, even manipulated a little, and that made any individual feel safer.[4] But it was infant need that had set it all off in the first place, and the natural behaviour of infants rather than adults that made the growth of spoken language possible.

Infancy was that period of life when doing things over and over again was fun. Such a period can be seen today in young non-verbal mammals, and of course in young humans. Anyone who has spent time with a two- or three-year old will know the feeling of desperation when faced with insistent demands for games, words, phrases and stories to be repeated ad nauseam. Young children, discovering that repetition is both enjoyable and rewarded by success, will persist in an activity long after adult enthusiasm for it has waned. Yet it is exactly this kind of dedication which fosters their early language development.

So also for the young Ergaster. Coordination, strength and ease came only with practice, whether it was walking, running, climbing or wielding a stick, and verbal activity was no different. Words were physical sensations and auditory sensations, and were amusing – again, just as they are today. Children love the sound and feel of words like "splish-splash", "wibbly-wobbly" "Gruffalo" "Laa-Laa" and so on – and practicing them is not a chore. If the syllables which carried meaning in early spoken language needed a strong root system to help them establish, then infancy was a veritable hothouse for it.

Non-specific vocalising may well have had a history of accompanying particular activities, and while life remained routine there was no pressure for innovation. The newer, specifically *verbal* activity would also work well as it was – until a challenge presented itself. Then verbal output was stretched to its limits, and under the pressure of the moment, and without thinking, a youngster's brain would cast about for help. That's when spoken language would grow – just a little.

~~~~~~~~

The family groups spent cautious weeks in the vicinity of the river, but as the water level dropped and the heat returned, the ground began to crack, forming angular shapes in the crusty earth. Plants wilted and toughened, and the haze made the
~~~~~~~~

horizon shimmer again; the Ergaster gathered themselves together and resumed their journey.

It was as ever, both opportunistic and purposive. As the months and years passed they took what the plain provided, or sought out areas of woodland. Sometimes they sat and observed the behaviour of the wildlife whose habits informed their understanding of the land and its climate, a process enhanced by words. If self-generated sound patterns could be superimposed onto the myriad of perceptions which made up the Ergaster view of the world, then the world became more manageable.

And this ability began to filter into their self-awareness. It added another dimension to the distinction between the animals they'd been long ago, and what they were becoming.

All of which was why, on one particular day, the word "*mahno?*" could be heard, at first said softly and urgently, and with the stressing and intonation of surprise. Among the groups making their way along the edge of a scrubby stand of trees, there was a sudden unity of attention, and a drawing closer.

During the years of wandering, inevitably particular groups had gone their own way and the composition of remaining families had altered. Some of their oldest members had died – few lived beyond fifty - some juvenile males had taken a risk too many, and one or two new-borns and their mothers had also been lost. This included the mother of the small female who had escaped the crocodiles. Following the usual pattern of four year gaps, she had become pregnant again during their time near the river, but hadn't fared well when, for a brief but crucial period, meat was not the prize it seemed. The plain had flattened out, and it took longer to reach the sloping hillsides where other kinds of food were available. For the same reason, the active males were committed to lengthier scavenging forays, and what was hacked from carcases and brought back was often fly-blown by the time it was eaten. To a developing foetus its toxins were disastrous,[5] and until evolution took account of the risk (and provided the possible safety mechanism of morning sickness), little could be done to avert the consequent demise of both mother and unborn child.

The young male, now eight years old, was still there though, being cared for by kin, and now he dodged under the bodies bending forward over a large swollen bole at the base of a vine. What he saw was surprising. A wide gash had split the bark, exposing a deep cavity in its interior.

Already there was a general movement away, the Ergaster searching ahead for the footprints showing which way whoever had damaged the vine had come and gone. But the traces had been erased by the frequent dust storms, and a closer look at the inside of the bole confirmed that its fibres were discoloured and dry; weeks had gone by since it had been opened up

One thing was certain, however. Although animals, such as antelope, tore and scraped at the bark of trees, none could make such a clean, neat split in the base of a vine; only another human, wielding a sharpened stone would leave such a scar, and only he had the dexterity to excavate its contents and squeeze out its store of moisture.

Sightings of one or two other hominin species were not infrequent, but there were differences of appearance and habit which kept them apart. If the small band of family groups could find the signs left by the Ergaster who had been here, they would follow and seek them out. Unlike some periods in the past, when larger wooded valleys and seasonal rainfall gave reliable foraging, the dry climatic conditions of the day led to hominin families becoming more vulnerable, exposed to danger and the risk of being underfed. They sensed that being in a larger group reduced their stress, driving predators off a kill succeeded better, and they had more mating opportunities.

So the techniques which the Ergaster hominins employed to track animals would now be used to search for their own kind, people who looked like themselves, behaved like themselves and sounded like themselves.

<table>
<tr><td>

The seedbed for spoken language...

- Consistent sound patterns (words) became familiar through the natural repetitiveness of infant play and routine activities.

- Words could be composed of sounds bearing no relationship to an outside stimulus – familiarity alone imposed a meaning.

- The meaning of one word was enhanced when another was linked to it.

- Experiences could be recorded by using words.

- Recalling information was helped by such memories.

</td></tr>
</table>

CHAPTER 7

Reaching a Wider Audience

Homo ergaster…1.7million years ago – continued.

Like the scarred vine, there would be evidence left by the hominins ahead of them. A search among bushes a short way east had revealed dung containing the undigested seeds of berries favoured by the hominins, so it was certain they were going in the same direction. Sometimes tool flakes were found, sometimes smoothed sleeping areas, but often days went by with no trace of the others at all.

The families had also to seek out food sources for themselves, and the pressure to cope with both tasks heightened the hominins' attentiveness to surroundings in all directions. The land had flattened to the north, and in the thickly forested hills to the south they discovered huge baobab trees with their strange oval fruit. Then came a day when unusual birds added interest to a sky flecked with unfamiliar clouds, and the wind blowing towards them smelt fresh even though it carried no rain.

So they slowed, although what was about to confront them was likely to tug them forward, and the hominins were likely to comply. Deep-seated impulses often worked as imperceptible guides, helping them sense such things as plants that were safe to eat, which ones had properties that eased pain and discomfort, and equally, perhaps by colour or smell, when something ought to be avoided.[1] In this instance the urge they felt was a positive one, lifting their confidence, and they finally drew to a halt as they did when moods were shared. Some found a tree to climb, and got a better look at the vista opening out.

The immense curve of the horizon ahead, smooth and apparently clear of trees was puzzling. But it was still a great way off, and between it and themselves there was something that had to be investigated.

They pushed on, hurrying, and gradually the object of their interest became clearer. Birds could be seen in a restless tumult of confusion, wheeling and screaming, skimming and plunging into a vast, open lagoon. Reed beds and low bushes surrounded it along a perimeter of wide bays and narrow inlets, and although it was unlike any waterhole, lake or river in their experience, everything about it was a demonstration that food here was abundant.

For some days they almost forgot about the other hominins, needing to fix in their minds an image of the layout of the place, so that they could recognise specific landmarks, the location of safe retreats and the places where freshwater streams fed into the lagoon. Then, later, foraging in familiar fashion would include a more extensive examination of what was new here.

And what was here was fish, and, of course, the birds. The more they ventured into the shallow lagoon the richer its hoard appeared to be. Apart from shoals of small fry, dark-shelled mussels clustered by the banks – easy pickings and soon prised open with sharpened sticks. Then there were the shrimps which even the youngest juveniles could catch once they'd learned to spot their pale forms below the surface. Equally novel were the sediment-dwelling fish, sudden squirmings felt as hominin feet disturbed them. The larger fish eluded the Ergaster, but another bounty was the birdlife. Some species grazed on the banks, and these could be taken easily by approaching quietly then stoning or clubbing.

The other Ergaster had also been here, leaving tracks of broken reeds and piles of shells and bones. And late one day they could be seen in the distance, unmistakeable, upright forms like themselves.

~~~~~~~~

Their appearance itself bore witness to the demands of their history. Fossil remains of *Homo ergaster* show a range of physical changes that relate to the climate and to their reliance on being bipedal, but by looking for features known to be involved in the act of talking it's also possible to suggest how capably these hominins might have been producing speech.

For a start, the way the skull sat on top of the spine was different. In *Homo habilis* its base had been flat, and by the time of *Homo sapiens* it had become highly flexed, but in *Homo ergaster* it was somewhere in between. So this slight doming was creating a chamber above the larynx, at the top of the throat. It was the pharynx, and would have quite an effect on any sounds and syllables an individual uttered.[2]

Vocal communication started off in the larynx, sounds being created by the vocal cords, a parallel pair of flexible cartilages stretched over the top end of the trachea (the tube through which air passes to and from the lungs). Whenever breathing out coincided with an impulse to vocalize, these cords
~~~~~~~~

would close together, interrupting the breath stream, vibrating and causing a note whose pitch would vary depending on how tense the vocal cords were.

In Ergaster hominins, this note could now resonate inside the pharynx – that extra space under the base of the skull – and the voice it created would have displayed a richer quality compared to that of all the hominins who went before. If *Homo ergaster* was edging towards human behaviour patterns, he would also be the first whose voice was beginning to sound human too.

That voice, however, wasn't simply a note with pitch that was sonorous. As in other animals, the mouth was also a resonating chamber for the voice, but in the Ergaster it was one which was able to change shape inside. The vital ingredients for increasingly meaningful vocal communication were increasingly different sounds, and these were the direct result of movements made in and by the mouth.[3] The tongue was shorter. Its root was lower because the larynx had become lower, and this gave it more freedom of movement than the thick high tongue of earlier hominins. It might now flatten, bunch, bang and click. At the same time, the lips could open, close, spread and relax, and at the back of the nose a small muscular flap, the uvula, could momentarily open or close it off, influencing how 'nasal' the voice sounded. The cheek teeth were smaller, and as the jaw widened allowing the stream of sounds to flow out, the result of these alterations in shape was to create variety.

Technically, each sound would have its own characteristic acoustic frequency. The brain recognised each wavelength as belonging to 'b' or 'g', 'oo' or 'ee',[4] 'm' or 'n' – or 'p' and 'k', the quieter sounds which slipped in when the voice, just for an instant, switched itself off. Syllables would have their own particular pattern: words would have theirs.

With the richer resonance and greater amplitude that the pharynx supplied, self-expression could really capitalise on such features, because the value of adding and establishing more sounds was that the repertoire of possible combinations got bigger. More syllables could arise and so could more words. The list of sounds, syllables and words would still have been small compared to ours today - but for all that, why had it been increasing at all?

If hominin environments and experiences had remained static, there'd have been no need for any expansion of calls, or utterances, syllables or words – the pressure to utilise and enhance oral innovations simply wouldn't have been there. Over thousands of years, though, as the Afarensis, then Habilis, then Ergaster changed what they did to survive, the variety of life could be reflected vocally - as long as there were enough sounds to create different patterns. The process wasn't deliberate, of course. Any chance vocalisation of daily life could assume a more consistent form if used often enough in the same circumstances, and there was always the old underlying communication system of non-vocal signals to help make the meaning clear.

With such use then, there was bound to be pressure on the muscles to become adept, and on nervous pathways to consolidate and drive the system. What would become 'the vocal tract' had begun in mechanisms designed for feeding and breathing, but they could modify themselves for another purpose if required. And clearly this was required, or we wouldn't have become the species that spoke.

One aspect of the modifications had come at a price, though.

A larynx situated lower down, as the Ergasters' was, carried the risk of choking to death.[5] In our primate cousins it has stayed high up - allowing them to safely breathe and swallow at the same time - so what excuse could there have been for inflicting such a hazard on our ancestors? The legacy of a possible aquatic period in the distant past – the low larynx enabling some mammals to swim – seemed to have been retained, yet once hominins resumed a life on dry land, the original, pressing reason for the adaptation no longer applied. It was surely hardly worth keeping just on the off-chance that submerging might come in handy once in a while. What's more, the larynx began to descend into its lower position during infancy – did that really make sense? Well it would if evolution was finding that spoken language was so important to infant survival that the risk of choking was being outweighed.

~~~~~~~~

There was no possibility of catching up with the Ergaster group ahead of them on that first day, and once the excitement had died down a little, the small company of families tried to return to the normal routines of bedding down for the night. Young individuals, however, those on the cusp between babyhood and infancy, had picked up on the mood and were reluctant to settle.

Bound normally to stay close to mothers and carers for food and safety, they were also becoming
~~~~~~~~

aware of what lay further away, and curiosity *had* to be satisfied. Down by the lagoon there was a great deal to be curious about.

Right at the water's edge one small hominin was watching something he'd never seen before. He was standing in a boggy patch surrounded by clumps of rushes, and had been pressing his toes into the mud, seeing how it slowly rose and hid them. Suddenly the intrusion disturbed a frog, and its leap towards the vegetation, followed by its motionless efforts to avoid detection had set off squeals and a succession of demanding calls.

A juvenile ran across, listening to the infant's efforts as he pointed and struggled. There were just enough clues for the youngster to make a guess. He peered into the reeds. The pattern of sounds he uttered attached themselves to what the infant was focused on:

'Frog,' he said, 'frog jump… frog jump!'

They both observed the frog until it suddenly launched itself back into the water, and the infant now had a word for the animal plus another for what he'd seen it do. The little hominin went back to his game with the mud, repeating the words over and over. If he frightened another frog, this time he'd know what to say.

Bipedalism offered the infant Ergaster new experiences, and verbal language could twine itself around new sights and sounds in ways that rewarded his curiosity and helped him build and retrieve his store of information. Over his lifetime and the lifetime of his species, that would be a key to success – but the process had to start as soon as he began to explore.

As a baby, suckling at his mother's breast, the little hominin's larynx had been safely high in the neck, and could press against the epiglottis, a cartilage which would close off his windpipe and stop liquid getting in. Then, when he began to vocalise, playing with sounds after a feed, they were for his own amusement, being no more than soft babblings. When he began to make use of them to *communicate,* however, the larynx was starting its descent, and it made his pharynx longer.

Even just a little more resonance made his vocal efforts clearer to the wider audience beyond his mother's side. When he crawled, when he tried his first unsteady steps, when he took off to investigate the world around him, in addition to the loud alarm call he used in emergencies, he had highly audible sounds and syllables available for other situations. By puberty the larynx would have settled, and when he grew to adulthood his voice would enjoy the resonance of that elongated pharynx - and there was also the benefit that the low larynx made panting easier when he started to run.

But he might still choke, despite the 'false cords' - elastic tissue which narrowed the opening between the pharynx and the larynx whenever he ate or drank.

The low larynx was here to stay, though, and its retention may well have been driven by infants: it was their vocal efforts that were being enhanced, in synchrony with their forays into a wider world.

When morning came the Ergaster group had to find a way round the lagoon towards the strangers. Its surrounding salt marshes were a wilderness of waterways and channels, but making contact had become a powerful if apprehensive compulsion, so they pressed on, taking short cuts across bays where they felt safe. When disturbed like this, the flocks of wildfowl would rise up in great masses, momentarily shocking the hominins with their sudden explosion of wings and calls. Each inlet and creek seemed to erupt as they approached, and it was these sounds carrying across the water which attracted the attention of the other Ergaster, who until now had been unaware that they were being followed.

At the sight of each other, even so far off, the responses which welled up were of intense excitement. There was a crescendo of calling and shouting, and raising of arms. Each group picked its route through the startled wildfowl until within a few yards of each other, and a process of cautious acquaintance began.The Ergaster had descended from social animals, and there were rituals of greeting that no doubt owed much to those primate origins, being both physical and vocal. Now these might include verbal elements too - the highly meaningful sound combinations which rose to prominence within the expressions they used.

That done, however, it would have been through the daily routines of foraging and resting that acceptance might take place, and valuable cooperative behaviours emerge.

~~~~~~~~

Understanding each other's communication during such activities would have been integral to the process, and despite initial unfamiliarity it might not have been too difficult. All being Ergaster hominins, they shared a way of looking at the world. And at this early stage, most of their utterances were so shaped by responses to its visible and audible impact they might well have had a core of expressions in common.
~~~~~~~~

However, at an individual level, tongues and lips might produce both vowels and consonants in slightly different ways, and the lilt of the voice could vary; so each group of families might have its own faint dialect. Alongside each other, and in the gatherings when they rested, however, their hearing stretched to interpret these variations, picking up on the context of what was happening, and on the visual clues from face, gesture and signs to confirm meaning. It was, after all, something they had done as infants and the technique would kick in again now.[6]

For all of them, the Ergaster lifestyle itself was creating fertile ground in which spoken language could grow. The hominins were moving through the landscape, and attention to animal behaviour was vital. Firstly they needed to avoid being attacked, secondly there were opportunities to scavenge from kills, and thirdly, with their tools, they were beginning to hunt more effectively.

So, like the various antelopes, zebra and wildebeest herds of the plains, hominins were watchful, instantly wary when any big cats ceased their deceptive, nonchalant padding at a distance. They registered the way the ears went back then the low, slow stalking stance; experience had taught them about the animals' intentions. And if no predators were visible, the Ergaster observed what the herds were doing. If they were relaxed and browsing, well and good, but if they stopped suddenly, heads up and nostrils twitching, that put the hominins on their guard. Unlike the herds, speed of escape wasn't an option for them. So the Ergaster had become reliant on spotting these early warning signs, interpreting the slightest change in behaviour or attitude – sensing what might be going on in an animal's mind – and recognising weakness.

It was feeding into their own increasing capacity to hunt, but it worked with each other too; it would be another dimension in their dealings with one another. If Ergaster infants had to be quick to learn what was useful, then this certainly qualified. Hominin behaviour would have its moods and patterns, needing observation and interpretation for interactions and relationships to be successful - and they would certainly employ this kind of 'theory of mind' in their behaviour and communication with newcomers.[7]

~~~~~~~~

Sorting out relationships was happening very easily indeed among the young of the two groups. Because they vocalised more freely, any verbal element would have been very much part of the process. Their play had similarities, and it was through this that much of the groundwork was done. Initially they kept their distance but it wasn't long before physical exploits merged in and around the lagoon, becoming both noisy and productive.

Receptive and youthful brains, predisposed to filter out the flimsiest niceties of any sound from the environment, applied the same skills to the vocal nuances of their playmates. Their ears coped with a certain range of differences, and made leaps to understand.[8] Then their pronunciation began to synchronise, each influencing the other, so that soon they would sound alike. All of them had a general underlying tendency to conform (it was a prudent move if you were small and wanted to
~~~~~~~~

avoid trouble) and their vocal behaviour was no exception.[9]

What Ergaster infants said as they engaged in the chasing or climbing or mock-fighting games was often simply self-expressive vocalising, but when some manipulation was called for, their communication was just a verbal extension of the power they had wielded when they were very young. Utterances might include within them meaningful patterns conveying 'Come', 'go', 'stop', 'get', 'throw', 'sit', 'give'…….;[10] And with playmates whose hierarchies had been negotiated somewhere else, the bays, inlets and grassy margins were a ferment of sizing up and finding ways to lever for position. All the young tested not only their physical muscle but threw their burgeoning verbal weight around too. Such practice equipped them for the kind of manoeuvrings that were taking place among the older Ergaster.

In a new environment something else was happening too. Unfamiliar animals or plants – even features of the landscape – had no name. And when adults weren't forthcoming there was nothing to stop the young from labelling things themselves. They could use syllables they'd played about with, and if consistently applied to the same things, such words could easily become part of everyone's vocabulary.

~~~~~~~~

This sort of thing still goes on even today – although you'd assume everything there is to know would have been officially identified by now. Yet how often do small children invent their own name for a
~~~~~~~~

special toy? (Until recently a mouldering creature called Gaddy resided in my loft.) And children's imaginary friends can have imaginary names too – Chelery, Twingle Twanx and Cowmitt all appear in a recent study of the topic. It may be only a small glimmer, but their originality and appealing sound bear witness to children's continuing creativity – given half a chance.

~~~~~~~~~

Perhaps the young Ergaster made up names for some of the new foodstuffs being found. There was certainly enough for all the families, so time could be spent resting. They clustered under the fringe of palm trees growing some way back from the margins of the lagoons, and during these periods physical and vocal grooming – "stroking" – broke barriers and helped satisfy curiosity. The two Ergaster groups began to relax with each other. They delved for whatever responses the brain had come up with in the past, and nudged them into improvising some more for the present. As before, vocal communication performed in its own resourceful way – not a separate, intellectual entity, "out there" to be selected for use, but an integral aspect of the behaviour that typified the Ergaster lifestyle. It was as uninhibited as any animal call, provoked by situations, and prone to repetitions as long and as often as a situation lasted – which was helpful; this was precisely the sort of thing that established verbal language as a habit.

Under the palm trees the Ergaster were building the kind of links and relationships which strengthened the position of their species in the habitat they occupied. The seasons came and
~~~~~~~~~

went, replenishing the lagoon with fish and fowl and it was only when the group size had expanded through the addition of new generations that pressures mounted.

Some families would join together and break away. They were well-fed, strong, and had had time to form firm bonds; they were large enough in number to move on and answer those deep-seated impulses to explore.

Preliminary forays towards the elusive curved horizon had identified few challenges, and so there came a day when a new group did not return.

They had left the lagoons and waterways behind, following a line of hills that led tantalizingly in the direction of the wide curved horizon, and at the end of one afternoon the hominins came to where wooded slopes merged into a wide band of tall palm trees. The vegetation stretched unbroken as far as the eye could see, with pale sand fringing its outer edge. Beyond that was only water, and that too spread out and away, as far as the eye could see.

The Ergaster families stopped and their minds took it all in, evaluating it, assessing whether it offered possibilities. With the heaviest of their shaped tools they broke open the palm nuts littering the ground, glad of the liquid inside, using thinner flakes to get out the delicate white flesh. Then, when night fell, they sat and let tensions subside. Perhaps too they hit on syllables that expressed how they'd seen the vastness of the ocean, and how they'd felt the rhythm of its pounding waves.

<u>The seedbed for spoken language...</u>
- Anatomical adaptations to the larynx enhanced verbal output.
- Verbal skills benefited from trends towards increasingly cooperative behaviour.
- Greater interdependence increased the opportunities for longer and closer social interactions.
- Having to understand the subtle signs that animals displayed set the scene for more insightful human communication.

CHAPTER 8

An Expanding Organisation

Home ergaster (continued)…1.5 million years ago.

It's easy to imagine *Homo ergaster* groups reaching the sea during the course of their wanderings, but did they spend time there? It's difficult to prove. The shifting waves have ensured that traces of occupation are unlikely to be found: ice sheets melt, the earth shrugs its seismic shoulders and coastlines realign to accommodate the sweeping tides.

Yet there is one thing. By about 1.5 million years ago, *Homo ergaster* hominins possessed brains that at 900cc were almost a third larger than their Habilis predecessors[1] and it's possible they did owe that, in part, to the sea.

Hominins had already spent several hundreds of thousands of years getting to grips with life in the Great Rift Valley and, latterly, on its surrounding grasslands. The pressures had provoked brain reorganisation and brain growth – redundant parts were recruited while other areas expanded. As time went by, reliance on these bigger brains also meant that hominins hungered for those foods which would provide the right sort of energy to keep them working. And what brains needed in particular was Omega-6 and Omega-3 fatty acids – especially Omega-3.[2]

Out on the grasslands some nuts, leaves and seeds offered a limited amount of Omega-3, but by far its richest source of supply would be seafood.

So, when Ergaster groups did arrive where land met sea and sky, what did they make of that ebb and flow of seething water, its translucence, its colour, its bays and headlands? Whatever the immediate reaction, exploring families would have used both curiosity and experience to identify the likely locations of food – they had out-performed the primates who could focus only on finding a particular kind of fruit or flower. So in tidal rock pools they could grope beneath rocky ledges for crabs or shellfish. Along the shoreline larger fish would sometimes be washed up after a storm, and the silt of estuaries would yield mudskippers. Where there were mangrove swamps, oysters could be found in abundance, clinging to their tough arching roots.

Maybe too Ergaster look-outs saw fewer signs of the predatory animals they feared. By the sea, even the frail and the young could find food with relative ease; the general health of everyone would benefit.

So if they stayed, for how long? Long enough to give brain growth the boost which made it bigger? This was a new environment, unlike those to which they were adapted and it might well tax their ingenuity and demand yet more from the power-house on which they depended. For even into adulthood, flexibility mattered.[3] Whenever adversities were consistently overcome, those innovative approaches which had led to success would be reflected in the way neural pathways were inclined to mesh in the brain. Individuals, whose genetic make-up had, from birth, predisposed them to do well, would determine how well the species as a whole did. And time and again over the generations they altered behaviours, pushing out the boundaries of their cognitive capabilities.

Whether they sensed it or not, the coast had a lot to offer. A diet high in the nutrients provided by seafood might be both satisfying and stimulating, and not just in relation to brain growth and function. Fertility would have been enhanced by the iodine present in marine creatures and in seaweed, so perhaps the population of hominins grew too.[4]

If such a habitat could indeed be conquered and added to the range of places hominins occupied, then other opportunities were opening up. A healthy, reproductive population might have the motivation to go to the next bay, reach the furthest headland, cross wide inlets when the tide was low.[5] The Ergaster were doing something new - moving within the continent of Africa but also emigrating beyond it.

Or maybe the picture was much starker. When the climate was working against them, what alternative did they have except to range further and further in search of plants and animals on which to feed? These long-distance travellers who reached parts of Russia, India and even the Far East[6] might instead have been the hardy remnants of a population on the brink - the tough who got going, and kept going.[7]

Whatever the reasons for their dispersal, however, by about a million years ago the Ergaster had already gone way beyond the land in which they'd originated, and their variation of the species would come to be known as *Homo erectus*.

But for the Ergaster who stayed behind in Africa's interior, the ancestors of our own species, what circumstances provided the kind of conditions in which language might grow yet more shoots and branches? In particular, what was making such a profound impression on our evolution that childhood continues to this day to be the only ground in which it can truly begin to flourish?

~~~~~~~~~

The young juvenile had become bored with his playmates and was edging towards a group of half a dozen adult males squatting under the branches of a huge flat-topped acacia tree. At eight years old he was starting to wean himself from the company of younger kin and the females, showing interest in the different activities of the males.

Detecting his approach, they glanced round at him. He was slim and long-legged, and might one day be about 1.63 metres tall – a build which would allow him to cope with the heat and the long distances demanded by a savannah lifestyle.[8] His face was dominated by ridges on his brow, and jaws which projected forwards, and although his cheek teeth – when the adult ones had finished coming through – would be modest in size, his upper incisors were strong and shovelled, ready for gripping and tearing. He had a low forehead, and most noticeable of all, a prominent nose, with nostrils angled downwards. The Ergaster had the stature and proportions of many living humans, and they might, from a distance, be viewed as men, women and children.

When the boy spoke, it was in waves of short phrases. His chest was barrel-shaped – no longer wide at its base after meat-eating had reduced the space needed for intestines - but it was as yet too sparsely supplied with nerves to sustain prolonged speech. He could nonetheless combine and recombine brief verbal expressions to make a case for himself in most situations.[9] To him, however, the
~~~~~~~~~

idea that what he said were 'words' and 'phrases' did not exist; he was 'calling' like other animals; human calls were just characteristic of their species. The difference was qualitative – his communication system reached deep into the richness of his perceptions and came up with ways of representing them audibly. The distinctiveness of his call was down to the variety of his sounds, and his ability to group them in particular patterns.

For all the Ergaster, whether child or adult, in any act of 'speaking' it was the output as a whole which mattered – individual groups (words and phrases) were simply its more emphasised (and therefore more meaningful) bits.

The harmony of the men's voices rose and fell with an easy fluency, for with a maturing body had come features which liberated vocal activity a little more. They worked much as the stable physique of a man in his prime gave him the edge over youth when it came to stamina, or throwing with accuracy, or making precise changes of angle when stone-knapping. As far as speech was concerned, strong muscles and ligaments took full advantage of the space the lowered, post-pubescent larynx provided. An adult vocabulary, however, might have differed only slightly from that of a juvenile, because words related to a common lifestyle experienced by everyone every day. Youngsters picked up expressions whenever their interest was aroused. As was the case here.

The boy was drawn by the sound of the men's voices and the gestures accompanying them. He held back, then sidled quietly in beside the younger of his two uncles, listening to the phrases passing around and watching each face for its reaction. The nearby lake, the buffalo thorn bushes, and a baboon rock were mentioned and mentioned again. He knew the places that were referred to, having been to each one, and was aware that if the men were going to scavenge or hunt they always went over and over a list of locations in this way as they were deciding to set out.

But he'd not been with them on one of their long forays, and couldn't visualise the route in the way the men could. One day recently, he *had* recognised a route - it had needed only two features to identify it so was easier to recall; it was nearby, and a source of good stones. So he'd stuck close to his uncle and helped bring some of the cores back to their base, carrying them in a length of hide softened by beating. As he got older the men would be more accepting of his company and he'd learn to hold more place names in his memory – in the right order – so that he could venture further afield with confidence. The *sequence* was the important thing, because how would he make his way to and from a variety of places if landmarks were muddled in his mind?[10] How would he find his way back to the safe bases the group occupied from time to time? For the present, his inexperience made him a liability, but he was unconsciously preparing by recording as much as he could of what he saw and heard.

The boy's interest in an imminent trek was interrupted by hearing his name called. He responded with a quick 'Ha!' of acknowledgement, rising off his haunches and quickly scanning the other shady areas for the owner of the voice.

"Maneno, Maneno!"

The word meant 'talker' and had attached itself to him as he grew up – he'd vocalised early and picked up the useful sound-clusters with ease.

The call came again. It was high and insistent, and there was no ignoring it; reluctantly he left the acacia tree and crossed a patch of bare earth to where his small cousin was standing all alone.

She was about three years old, and spent much of her time near her mother, which also meant, of course, being part of a circle of largely female kin and their offspring.

The slow drift from place to place typical of previous hominins might now sometimes be replaced by a longer occupation of habitats[11] and although it was a lifestyle obedient to the seasons and the vagaries of the climate, pregnant women and the new-born would have benefited from the short time of stability this offered. Before Tatu was born, having kin nearby had helped to ensure that her mother would have enough food to take the baby to full term. The baby would grow inside her until its demands for nutrition were more than she could supply;[12] then it would be delivered and its rate of development slow down. But like all Ergaster babies, Tatu was born at a much earlier stage of neurological development than her chimpanzee cousins; to match their levels of ability at birth her mother would have been obliged to carry her for eighteen or twenty months – way beyond the energy limits for hominins.

So instead Tatu arrived with uncoordinated limbs and eyes that blinked and struggled to focus. She couldn't even cling to her mother herself, and would be intensely dependent on care-givers for her every need. Soon she was passed around and examined, and grew used to the rocking and gentle swaying which everyone did by instinct and which kept her calm. This way she became acquainted with the individuality of each person, their smell and especially their voices – her trust in the people around her was critical if she was to stay secure.

More to the point, however, the sensations she experienced through being touched and handled, and the movements she felt prepared her nervous system well for all the fine muscular activities which she would soon begin to develop, making up for her premature arrival. Deep in the brain, her vestibular system – the mechanism responsible for balance and posture[13] – had now done all that would ever be necessary for a two-legged human to maintain an upright stance; so one day she would master the art of walking, and although she might climb trees in play, there was no part of her brain which would tell her limbs to swing through a forest canopy.

Tatu would live on the ground, a dangerous place to be. So her brain fizzed with every task that would help her to stay alive, and right now it was brimming with eagerness for Maneno to take her *anywhere*. He was now good at foraging locally, and his excitement when he found things to eat rubbed off on Tatu – his reactions grabbed her attention: it was more fun with him than with the women.

So Maneno set off towards a tangled thicket and quickly found a grub making holes in leaves.

"Bite head," he said. It was a phrase that simply accompanied his action – he'd absorbed it originally when, as a very small child, he'd been trailing after his mother.

Tatu copied the phrase. For both of them it was a self-commentary, but incidentally it acted like an instruction for Tatu.[14] Then she grimaced.

"Not like," she said.

Maneno responded with a play face, and leading her to a grassy clearing, found a patch of little tubers. They both sat crunching the flesh, with Tatu repeating the name he'd used for them, pulling at the long green shoots that had provided the clue to where they were. She was learning from him – not just about food, but about the words which helped fix the day's activities in her mind – learning the acoustic signatures of each sound, and the order in which they were arranged. And, having had more practice, he was better able to blend the sound patterns together, so hearing him speak helped fine-tune her own efforts.

Suddenly they were distracted by a noisy commotion coming from the family groups – voices had an irresistible attraction – so the children scrambled away, Maneno pulling Tatu along so that she wouldn't get left behind.

There were often bursts of calling and verbalising within the group. Vocal communication may have taken on a greater role, but it hadn't replaced the old instinctive, physical responses to challenges, or fear, or excitement. These still rose to the surface just as they'd always done, and expressive language would inevitably reflect whatever emotions flared up too.

~~~~~~~~

If there was a trend for more families to join forces, then there were going to be wider variations in attitude to what was done, who with, and how to do it. And patterns of dominance had altered, so styles of communication, inseparable from such interactions, would express shades of conflict and of consensus.

More than that though, social situations, where involvement in activities was essential, were what
~~~~~~~~

may have driven changes in the way the brain organised itself. Cognitive development thrived in a company composed of individuals who differed, and it was the process of having to cope that drove valuable adjustments - the turmoil of contention may have been uncomfortable, but it *was* beneficial.[15]

In fact, the answers to many of the challenges hominins had faced historically had probably been down to individuals whose slight differences had given them an advantage. They'd had some genetic trait which worked better in certain situations, and it had spread through their descendants to become a species asset. But the system could also be responsible for another helpful phenomenon – specialisation. There would be those with greater aptitude for doing what the social group needed, and with time, this might result in tasks being undertaken, not necessarily by everyone, but by those who could do them best.

Quite apart from the broad male/female division of labour - a consequence of the females' long-term preoccupation with their young as much as of the males' greater power, there were other aspects of daily life which might tend towards specialisation.

For one thing there was the tool-making.

It was at around this time, with the emergence of *Homo ergaster*, that a new phase is evident in the making of stone tools – those outward and visible signs of an organised mind at work. What was being created were hand-axes, cleavers and bifaces – stones flaked on two sides that intersected.[16] These were tools deliberately shaped for specific purposes, exhibiting an emerging elegance and a consistency of form, even though their makers were separated by thousands of years and thousands of miles. It was how the brain of this human species approached the task that determined what the tools looked like, and it was a brain that had been evolving in response to a multitude of experiences.

Many of the simpler tools could probably be struck quite quickly without the need for particular strength, and were perhaps made by anyone. But larger tools and those that required specific shaping were another matter. The raw materials – maybe lava or quartz - behaved differently, so to develop the understanding and expertise to create the desired form would take time, and people with patience.

There was also tool-using. Maybe the women used heavy stones and sharp flakes to crush and chop food for their infants so that digestion was easier. If it was the men who butchered the meat with their heavy cleavers, would it be the women who wielded the sharp scrapers to remove residue and fur from hides? Once cleaned, animal skins could be softened a little by pounding and then used as extra protection to shield fragile new-borns from the worst of the elements and the tough dry vegetation that surrounded them.

In either sex, sometimes it was just the way the brain worked that marked out this or that person. Given the necessity of getting the most out of every habitat, anyone with a flair for spotting worthwhile features in a landscape would be attentive when the families were on the move, and when they lingered, a reliable knowledge of plant attributes – in addition to their edibility - was valuable. Some species of wildlife can identify mineral sources which have health benefits, and there is no reason to suppose that early humans lacked such a skill.

Adding an ability to give a name to this tree-bark or that kind of leaf or root would have helped consolidate the range of nutritional or medicinal properties the Ergaster could benefit from. Over time it would become an inventory that could be retrieved from the memory, and injuries and illnesses might be treated so long as someone in the family knew what to look for, could remember the kind of places it grew, and how it was used. Better still, with vocal communication, that knowledge could be passed around – and passed on.

Behind all this, of course, was the adult brain, quite a large adult brain. In contrast, the new-born Ergaster infant would arrive in a perilously premature state, so something had to happen at some point by way of compensation. If, as may be possible, the Ergaster growth style was similar to that of present day humans, the infant brain probably obliged by almost tripling in size by the time a child was about three years old. In today's children what this stimulates throughout the cortex is a sort of rampant overgrowth of the cells which make links when learning occurs, and these are available to be utilised or trimmed back as appropriate.[17] It's what enables children to acquire so many skills so fast and with such apparent ease.

Including, of course, the features of spoken language.

~~~~~~~~~

Maneno and Tatu quickly took in which adults were at odds with each other, listening and watching from a safe distance. There was tension in the air, felt by all the families, so everyone stopped what
~~~~~~~~~

they were doing and only gradually resumed their occupations when the shouting and aggression were clearly dying down.

With a trek imminent, however, no-one was doing much over where the flint-knapping took place, and Maneno guessed it would now be easy to find some cores and a hammer stone to have a go himself. He made his way across and sat down in the dust. Picking up a stone, he turned it in his hand to register its shape – where it bulged and where it narrowed - trying to recognise where to strike it, as he had observed the men doing.

"Got 'tone," said Tatu as she came alongside.

"Yeah. Big stone".

He wished she'd go back to the women, but she was just too curious.

Maneno scrabbled around among some broken lumps of basalt - debris from a knapping session.

"More stone…….little stone," he said, putting one into her outstretched hand.

"Little…'tone…" echoed Tatu, her tongue not quite managing to produce the friction for the sound at the beginning of the word. Being older, Maneno's finer coordination meant he was well able to say all the words in the mature Ergaster vocabulary, the fruits of a process that had happened slowly, over many generations. Hominin lifestyles had made demands on self-expression, and with their more agile tongues, older individuals had used the wider variety of sounds at their disposal in creating the new words they needed – but their very young had always lagged behind for a while.

So it was now, and Tatu benefited unconsciously from Maneno's example. It was as though he was up a tree, leaning down, offering a hand up to the higher branch where he was sitting.

She was already adept at combining simple vowels and consonants, but some finer sound combinations were still physically too hard. Nevertheless, her brain would store auditory patterns, so that she would go on aiming to say them as Maneno had done. And with just a little more agility, sooner or later her tongue would groove itself then swiftly flatten for the high-pitched sound that began how he had said "stone" - but she would be quite unaware of the orchestration of recall, matching and flurry of neuro-muscular activity which had gone into its achievement.

The boy was keen to have a go at knapping by himself, so he distracted Tatu by giving her a large stone and then coaxing her towards where her mother and friends were sorting through animal bones. Some of these were small, slender and sharp, and could be used to prise morsels of food from reluctant shells or seed cases. He pointed to the stone he'd given her, then to the cracked femur shaft one of the women had discarded.

"Big stone... big bone," he said to Tatu, making the last syllable stand out, knowing that his cousin would pick up on the rhyme; the effect was as though her hearing had just been tickled. A gurgle of delight rose in her throat and she squatted down.

"Big 'tone, big bone," she repeated, at once engaged in the verbal game and watching the work of sorting. The verbal game took off, turning into a sort of repetitious song; somehow the rhythms of words and phrases latched onto tunes in ways that helped her to remember them. It would be a habit to hold on to.

The women joined in her sing-song of sounds and words, keeping her interest, and Maneno took off back to his flint-knappping practice. Now Tatu would pick up vocabulary from the women, associating it with the practical skills she too would need to lean from those around her. The Ergaster, as a species, had found advantage in staying focused for longer periods; perhaps it was just the hunting, but equally likely, it could have grown out of taking the care necessary to fashion their tools. Infants now arrived with this potential, and their ability to learn – practical tasks and language – was greatly helped by being able to pay just a little more attention.

~~~~~~~~

So for Ergaster infants another asset was being added to the neurological flexibility that provided their solution to being born helpless. Throughout their infant years, while the brain's fibres and connections were at their densest, the options remained open for the young to learn whatever was necessary, and adapt easily in the face of need and challenge. When something they did consistently made a difference, valuable neural junctions and particular pathways would be well used. These would tend to be retained, allowing superfluous routes to disappear – a strategy that would concentrate energy and activity just where it could be most productive.

Whether the features which have become typically human were achieved swiftly, in spurts and starts, or whether they happened slowly and gradually is difficult to say; and maybe for both the Ergaster and the species which followed, it would take many generations to establish the timing and the particular order in which selected regions of the brain refined themselves in this way.
~~~~~~~~

In relation to better communication though – understanding and self-expression – the early years were exactly the right time to draw on this great well of neural abundance.

By the time Ergaster children were about three they would have been competent walkers, yet woefully inexperienced - quite incapable of fending for themselves as they got to grips with their world; learning from those around was vital. And the lifestyle of these hominins had aspects and complexities now that were too diverse to be merely observed and imitated.

The answer, of course, lay in the interplay between children and their social group that would be possible through language. Communication wasn't separate from all the behavioural changes that had accumulated over time, and it reflected the minutiae of everyday life. So situations, activities, encounters and events that generated communication in close kin fostered language development in children - their neural abundance meant that the facilities were there to develop wider comprehension and more effective expression.

It was all still carried along by way of the old familiar tunes, with intonation telling the mood or attitude of the speaker. As words and phrases emerged, the flow could be maintained through neutral vocalisations - much as today's speech is padded out with "I mean", "well", "like" and ums and ahs – unconsciously used and meaningless in themselves, but without which talking would feel jerky and stilted.

It was emphasis that drew attention to the most meaningful parts of an utterance. In longer calls these most salient features stood out like the highest contours in a landscape, their background being a mosaic of less specific vocalising, and infants would have no problem in focusing on these. And in the sort of situation Tatu mostly found herself, utterances would be short, said slowly with pauses, and she would, at nearly three, readily absorb something new every day.

~~~~~~~~

Suddenly, however, there was tension in the air again.

"Find waterbuck," said Tatu's father as he walked past Tatu and the women. It was another self-commentary, offering information.

Although the animals were large, their groups of six or seven females with young were often to be found grazing together. Also they calved at any time, so it wouldn't be difficult to harass some juveniles while mothers tried to protect those newly born. Once exhausted, separated and injured by missiles, the larger calves had little chance of escape.

There was a continuing hubbub as the men gathered stones and clubs or hand axes and started moving away from the trampled area of thickets. Tatu's mother had picked her up but, along with other infants she was getting agitated, pointing after the men, repeating "Papa go, Papa go," squinting at the low cloud of red dust that marked their departure.

When familiar figures weren't there it was as though infants suddenly felt the chill of abandonment, and were acutely aware of the men's absence. Dependence created strong bonds, but the women had the benefit of
~~~~~~~~

remembering past experience, and the words that would arise when they reappeared.

"Come back, come back," they murmured, and, more optimistically, "have meat, have meat.'

Infants joined in the calls, copying out of habit. When – if - the excursion was successful it would make sense, but for now just hearing and saying the phrases was a reassurance.

Little Tatu slid down from her mother, but her mood was still subdued, and with his instinct to divert her, Maneno took her by the hand to go in search of Hami. He was her ten year-old elder brother and Maneno too wanted more company. Also he had an idea that the three of them might have some fun together.

<u>The seedbed for spoken language…</u>

- Brain growth was stimulated by further expansion of habitats, and aided by marine sources of Omega-3.

- Lifestyle activities demanded sequencing ability and reliance on memory – both features involved in spoken language.

- Verbal communication responded to the challenge of increasing diversity within hominin groups, and benefited from resulting reorganisations within the brain.

- Greater ability to control attention facilitated learning generally and speech in particular.

- The neural abundance typical of infancy supported both the motor aspects of speech (articulation) and its semantic content (meaning), enabling each to develop quickly.

CHAPTER 9

One Thing after Another

Homo ergaster…1.5 million years ago - continued.

If the evolution of spoken language had been driven by survival challenges alone, this story might unfold as a catalogue of woes. But the main players were children, so there's far more to it than that. It didn't necessarily take a life-or-death emergency for an innovation to appear; the unknown was all over the place, and could be very exciting.

~~~~~~~~~

Hami was old enough and confident enough to go beyond the trampled areas used as a base, exploring a wider home range. This comprised a patch of land loosely defined by the lake, its grassland margins, euphorbia woods and a long rocky escarpment to the west. Usually he went with other youngsters, but sometimes it suited him to sneak off on his own; he enjoyed discovering for himself how to control fear, or work out how the animal in his sights might be stalked.

Today, however, Hami had been close enough to hear the commotion caused by the men leaving. Trying to deal with his own anxieties he was now hurling stones at a flock of guinea fowl pecking about in the scrub. Joining him, Maneno and Tatu did likewise until the creatures dispersed, and the rather pointless activity restored all of them to their former equable selves. They gradually began to wander further away from the base.
~~~~~~~~~

They were on a path made by Ergaster feet and therefore felt reasonably safe. In a social group with perhaps fifty members, there would nearly always be someone around ready to respond to alarm calls, especially those made by children. It was inevitable that young juveniles had to discover many facts about life for themselves, but the ties created within family groups ensured that adults would never quite lose the impulse to go to their aid.

The track would, the boys knew, take them to a particular stand of trees in which they might find small figs, so long as the monkeys hadn't already eaten them. Tatu just trotted along, keeping close to Hami. Behind her, Maneno was saying aloud what he saw on the way. It was how he was learning to fix the route in his head in the right order and Tatu in her turn soaked up the words and what they related to. She echoed him constantly, but when she herself named something she recognised, it was the boys who copied.

The buzzing of insects – even the dry rasp of their feet - faded into insignificance whenever their brains were selecting the sound of spoken language to listen to; for the time being its frequencies compelled their attention.[1]

As they approached the copse, however, all of them fell silent. They trod slowly and carefully, eyes and ears now focussed on any shape or sound that didn't quite fit. Their ability to focus on spoken language was still fed by an underlying skill - attending to what the natural world told them.

Reassuringly a pair of hornbills were preening their feathers high up in the fig tree, and below, in the grass at the edge of the undergrowth a flock of sparrows flitted and squabbled, scattering at the approach of the children. Hami pushed his way in, a brief flick of the hand telling Tatu and Maneno so far so good but take care. They followed a few paces behind, Tatu a little scared by where she was. Trying not to get snagged and scratched, they began looking for any fallen fruit.

"Stop!" The hissed command pulled them upright. Maneno and Tatu stiffened, holding their breath. Hami edged back to them, but his face was alight with excitement.

"Dog…. no… little…- little dog!" he whispered, pointing to where he'd just come through the bushes.

They frowned, uncertain, but he signalled to follow and with extreme care all three crept forward.

At first Maneno and Tatu could see nothing, despite Hami's pointing. Then as their eyes probed the leaf-litter, there it was, curled almost into a ball: a wild dog pup.

Fascinated, they stared, and suddenly the puppy sensed their presence, shifting its head, trembling. But it was too tiny to do more than begin a faint, thin whining. Hami reacted as he would have done to the cry of any helpless member of his family – he squatted down and gently lifted it up, cradling its warm body against his chest.

Maneno and Tatu reached out, touching it gingerly. The pup had been disturbed and resisted the strange sensation of being held, panicking and wriggling to avoid the stroking fingers. Its soft fur felt deeply pleasing, but its whines got louder, and just as Hami gave in, realising that the little animal wanted to be put down, he detected the unmistakeable sound of something trotting quickly through the dry vegetation towards where they stood.

Like lightning he thrust the pup back into its nest and shoved Maneno and Tatu sideways through the bushes, but made them stop almost at once with his finger to his lips saying "Shhh, shhhh…"

They peered through the tangle of twigs, struggling to make out the dappled coat of the female, approaching with her head down and nervous with hackles raised. She could smell them of course, but in her jaws was another tiny pup, and she dropped it before turning about, her big round ears twitching to find them.

With a quick jab in Maneno's ribs that said 'run!', Hami dived out of the copse as fast as he could, pulling Tatu with him. Over his shoulder he saw that the female, torn between chasing them off and guarding the pups she'd just moved, had opted to stand her ground and remain where she was,.

The three children regained the track back to the base, and only then did they slow to a panting walk.

Tatu's mind was in a whirl at what she'd seen, her excitement very evident to her mother and everyone who noticed the little group returning.

"What Tatu …?" queried her mother, arms extended to fold round and calm Tatu. But the child brushed them aside, barely able to contain herself.

"Dog… little dog!" she blurted, and her mother watched and waited. That wasn't all of it. Tatu had seen the dog packs hunting very recently, taking advantage of this dry season. What she'd never seen though was anyone holding a tiny dog in his hands, nor had she touched something wild alive, so warm and furry – and nor had she seen a dog carrying a living thing in its jaws.

"Hami – dog," she tried, and her mother studied Tatu's face.

"Hami, Hami…. hold!"… "Dog…little dog…"

Tatu began getting desperate, nearly crying with the compulsion to tell her mother about the extraordinary experience. It was like a rage.

With a supreme effort she raised her shoulders and took a great breath.

"Hami…hold…dog!"

Again, to get it across, "Hami. ….hold…..dog!"

Tatu's mother looked at Hami who was standing nearby. Delighted at what his sister had said, he nodded vigorously.

Encouraged, Tatu took another breath.

"Dog carry….dog carry… "It was difficult again. "Tatu see…. "

The effort of getting the words together in this way, as well as the fatigue which came from the afternoon's event was too much and she subsided, though the sparks in her mind were leaving tiny embers glowing. The brain was under pressure to come up with something new again.[2]

The next day, filled with energy, Tatu came out with:

"Tatu …. touch…dog."

It was an enlightened ordering of three facets of what had occurred – who was involved: herself, what she'd done: touched, and what she'd touched: dog. Tatu had already been managing phrases conveying two aspects of the events around her, but this connection was a leap forward.

Images kept coming back to Tatu, and she went on telling her mother and other family members, using the three-word verbal pattern. As it got easier, one evening, when everyone was sitting quietly she said,

"Dog carry… dog", using her hands to make the sign for little – one her family often used while foraging for fruit. They realised what she meant, and the thrill of success created another small glow in her brain.

~~~~~~~~

The Ergaster had long been acquainted with events which occurred in sequence – seasons, the acts of searching for food, preparing it, eating it, even the milestones of a life: birth, maturity, death. Hominins had also grown up understanding the implications of environmental sound sequences – the sudden clacking beak of a tree-top ibis, the instant swift slither down as the monkeys vanished, then the whisper of grass moving aside to let the leopard pass – danger! It was essential for them to draw conclusions from the particular order in which items of auditory information occurred.[3]

In the development of words and phrases, this facility had already contributed, allowing the consistent ordering of sound patterns to consistently convey hominin self-expression. But being able to grasp the implications of a particular procession of speech sounds depended entirely on the listener being able to remember a fleeting acoustic stimulus; so Ergaster spoken language came in short chunks which coped with their expressive needs and stayed within the limits of their auditory memory.

The words used would not, of course, have sounded like "stone", "hold", carry" or "dog". The Ergaster inventory of speech sounds would almost certainly have been alien to an English ear, probably containing clicks and consonants unlike any we say today, but if they conveyed meanings then the patterns were a form of human speech, one of many that would arise.
~~~~~~~~

As for the structure of a group of linked words, a new event with added dimensions which needed to be conveyed would threaten to spill over the edge of the usual phrase, and something both effective and compact was called for. In the youthful brain, charged up as it was, the networks branched and made connections,[4] and what they then created was the prototype for an utterance significantly different from what had gone before. It contained three units of information, and they were sequenced in a way that helped create an image in the mind of the listener. 'Hami carry dog' and 'Dog carry dog' were still quite short phrases – they'd have to be, if the ergaster breath control for speech was limited – but the device offered flexibility in how bits of information could be combined.

It was a useful technique, an embryonic grammar,[5] and its imprint would linger. Used again another day, and then again, the imprint would get firmer, contributing yet another microscopic rearrangement in the ultimate configuration of the brain, and opening up further possibilities for language to go on growing – if and when it needed to. Because it was like a stem reaching the point at which it could divide and branch, and if a stem could divide, then in their turn, so could the branches.

~~~~~~~~

Maneno's language was still able to grow, and in Tatu's company he too sometimes used the pattern of three-word phrases. His vocabulary was larger than hers, so he had more to play with, and more opportunities.
~~~~~~~~

When the hunting party returned several days later Maneno and Hami quickly occupied themselves with the tasks involved in dealing with the kills – fetching and carrying, gripping hard with their teeth to the ends of hides as the animals were skinned, trying their hand at using some of the smaller tools. Both watched and listened as adults spoke or fell silent.

The main kill had been the waterbuck, and Hami in particular could make a connection between the animal and where the men had gone to find it. During the recent trek to their present base he'd seen and smelt them near the lake, and he instantly associated the smell lingering from the carcase with the image in his mind. His brain was filing away information that prepared Hami for what he would need to know as he grew older. And it was categorising everything.

Hami's ancestors had unconsciously sorted landscapes as part of their exploitation of habitats, analysing subtle lines, shapes and colours. A range of mountains might be devoid of vegetation down to a certain level; a line of dense evergreen foliage might indicate river valleys; the point where the colour changed suggested deciduous woodland, and where the trees thinned and gave way to savannah the red earth would show through. Each triggered an interpretation hinting at sources of food, seasonal availability, ease or difficulty of terrain, and likelihood of dangers. The Ergaster were gaining an understanding of how the world worked, and it was helping them, as a species, to expand into new territories.

The process began very early. Surrounded since birth by the making and using of tools, Hami could probably already group them according to size and use. He would watch the men wield the huge, heavy axes whose weight and sharpness could drive through bone, and he'd see how they manipulated cleavers to prise joints apart. Maybe he too, once a carcase had been shared out, would use the small pointed picks for probing and reaching meat. Around him there would be scrapers for dealing with hide, acute edged flakes for cutting, rounded cobbles for grinding, smashing, and as missiles. Any young Ergaster in such surroundings would be grasping how his family dealt with the business of living, how they organised what they did.[6]

<center>~~~~~~~~</center>

Woven through all this activity and understanding, and part and parcel of the social dynamics of an ergaster life, vocal communication would have had to keep pace.

Putting it all together had resulted in these early humans expressing themselves not just through a typical primate system of emotion-driven calls and visible signs, but also by creating more specific representations of their world. Like their varied tools, they could achieve different effects when they shaped their utterances differently.

Dangers, food resources, significant colours, features of the environment, individuals and what was closest to them, their own bodies – anything that really mattered would now possess a discrete identity, to be held in the brain for instant use. A myriad of perceptions could metamorphose into speech.

But the Ergaster lifestyle was more complicated than that of their predecessors – it wasn't just landscapes and tools - every day was awash with interactions, including the complications which inevitably arose out of relationships within and between families. For a brain dedicated to keeping its owner out of trouble, confusion was not an option.

So as the brain set about classifying,[7] alongside the information being stored, and inseparable from it, would have been the words understood and uttered as hominins committed their perceptions to memory. Words too would be categorised. Like features of the natural world, they *behaved* in certain ways in a "locality" – they could influence other words around them. As words combined to form phrases, this would determine how spoken language shaped itself.

The brain, with its compulsion to make sense of what came in and what went out, was able to forge a relationship between the *kinds* of words which had to go together, and so the words weren't merely stabs at conveying something. There were subjects, actions, objects for the action, and the order in which these were heard could itself convey information.

Words had already amply demonstrated how much better communication worked when they came in tandem: 'more crocodiles', 'no fish', 'man *there!* It had helped when a person, an animal or a fruit could be described: 'old man', 'little antelope', 'fruit soft'. Names of things plus actions came up with results too: 'lion come', 'throw stone'.

Speech had to be connected if it was to be any use at all, so some mechanism had to arise which would avoid a lengthy trawl though every single word in the vocabulary. Categorising provided that mechanism. It meant the brain recognised that a descriptive word could go with a naming word: 'big egg', and a naming word could go with an action word: 'lion come'.

As additional words and phrases came on stream, and as soon as a phrase could contain three elements, spoken language would be able to rely on a hidden structure   growing with it, like an internal supporting network of fibres, which was sensitive to how words needed to relate to each other. It would allow a speaker to communicate at maximum efficiency with minimal effort.[8]

To a listening Ergaster hominin, these phrases were patterns composed of variable acoustic frequencies and changing duration; the trick being performed now was that all kinds of supplementary information could be gleaned by detecting when other units of meaning were being tacked on. What the Ergaster brain had been up to was devising very slick methods of connecting its inventories.

Clearly, Ergaster brains would have their work cut out dealing with this multi-faceted style of communication, as well as the usual everyday practicalities – so no wonder they were large. And no wonder also that Ergaster infants continued to be the ones on whom this made the most impact, with their long climb to reach an adult level of functioning.

Like the Ergaster, each new human species, with its advances and alterations, would present its two to three year-olds with the same challenge. And always the brain's dynamic contribution would continue to kick in with its generous supply of neurological resources. Mostly, of course, the children's situations would be routine so it was the firm pathways of everyday habits of communication which were being laid down. But every now and then some factor could cause pressure to mount and a new link would be forged in the busy networks. Spoken language would move a stage further – and not just for the individual child pushing against the limitations of his inheritance, but for the host of his descendants. Maybe sometimes advances came thick and fast.

~~~~~~~~

Maneno drifted easily between involvement in the daily tasks that he could help with, developing his own foraging skills, and playing with whoever felt so inclined. Inevitably, when Tatu gravitated towards him, the games would include the verbal ones she relished. His language systems were still eagerly receptive so he and his cousin would both stretch what they said and understood, just as they might for fun test elasticity in a length of sinew.

Their shared adventure had stuck in both their minds, and was easily retrieved by the phrases they'd used. But because of their flexibility, 'Like touch dog' had got the possibility of becoming 'Like touch *little* dog' or even, one day 'Big dog carry little dog'.

But perhaps not for a few hundred thousand years. It would be the restrictions of an unwilling rib cage, of breath control not quite ready for the innovation, which would decide how easily these more demanding utterances could establish themselves.

For Tatu, though, the simpler skill did come to her aid again, when Hami died.

The winter drought finally broke, one day when Hami was down at the edge of the lake. He had an abscess under a tooth and was feeling too
~~~~~~~~

miserable for company – and not alert enough to the weather. In a deluge of rain, streams suddenly gathered themselves together, tumbling over the escarpment, crashing and careering between boulders to take whatever low-lying route was available. Already trying to make his way back Hami fought to see through the driving rain. But his usual path had been obliterated and the grassland was a wilderness of angry rivers. Stumbling and slipping he simply disappeared.

Days later, when members of the group were searching the sodden ground, caught on a thorn bush they found the hide cloth in which he'd kept his hammer stone and flakes. Hami they never found. It would be a million and a half years before the lake's thick sediment gave up Nariokotome Boy, the name by which the skeleton of a young ergaster male would be known, found near Lake Turkana.[9]

Standing by the bush, and again, later, back at the camp, "Water kill Hami," said Tatu sadly, "water kill Hami."

- The capacity in this species for creating a variety of tool shapes to deal with specific tasks is evidence of the brain's ability to categorise - an essential feature in the development of language.

- Awareness of sequential events and an understanding of how an action produces an effect reflect the brain's ability to deal with things that combine with and influence each other – a necessary requirement for grammar (syntax) to emerge.

- Lengthening attention span (needed for tool making and hunting) made it possible for longer utterances to be used and listened to.

- Mature speech (more practised and better coordinated) differed from early speech, and infants' drive to copy continued to help them conform to the patterns used around them.

- Mobility exposed young children to new experiences demanding expression – a powerful factor in prompting the expansion of spoken language.

CHAPTER 10

People with Purpose

Late *Homo ergaster*…990,000 years ago.

The margins of Lake Turkana would flood and dry out many times during the lifetime of *Homo ergaster*. There had been a long period when interglacial episodes had tended to be more frequent, and when this happened the air was humid and very warm, and it had been a respite for the living landscape. Some trees and plants, along with the insects, reptiles, birds and mammals whose lives they supported had reclaimed territory lost in the dry years. Conditions might never quite return to their former state, though, because the scars were too deep and in some instances evolution couldn't unravel the changes that had taken place.

Perhaps some Ergaster families struggled to cope too. By about 400,000 years ago a new species had taken over - with more brain-power at its disposal, and with the ability to make yet more sophisticated tools. They were early *Homo sapiens*, *almost* our own kind and they too would have the cognitive and anatomical potential to communicate through spoken language.

So what had happened to the Ergaster? If a particular genetic advantage in a particular family or group meant they survived when their neighbours fell by the wayside, it would be their members who reproduced to become dominant, and a new species would begin to evolve. Or maybe in the tough times populations became separated, and it was only one branch that was able to continue, evolving in isolation as it responded to the challenges of the day.

Whatever the case, as the sun went down on the Ergaster, changes in behaviour might give hints as to what would emerge in their successors. There are, however, precious few signs of late Ergaster, and without solid evidence it's hard to know what they were doing.

But there are two intriguing examples of behaviour which left their mark in the fossil record at around 990,000 years ago, and these do give us the chance to hazard a guess about the circumstances surrounding each of them, and to catch a glimpse of what might have been going on in the late Ergaster mind, and the role being played by spoken language...

What happened took place at Olorgesailie, many hundreds of miles south of Lake Turkana, in the eastern branch of the Great Rift Valley, about mid-way between two high mountain ranges.

~~~~~~~~

The area was inhabited by a number of late Ergaster clans, each one composed of five or six families and possibly totalling a hundred or more individuals;[1] the trend of Ergaster groups to form coalitions – to coordinate the manner in which they met life's challenges – had gathered strength, and these closer bonded companies would become the norm.

Such groups would have descended from successful families who had lived in the region for many years, and they understood its hills and plains, and its sometimes unpredictable moods. Families passed on to each new generation a
~~~~~~~~

knowledge of how to live off the plants and animals around them, and where to find the resources they needed for their tools.

And their skill was not simply in shaping and using these artefacts; they had an eye for the range of stone from which they could be made. Up to seventeen different kinds might be involved, and to reach such specific rocks as these would require a sense of purpose, and someone to lead the way.

Kifimbo was such a guide. His clan's home base was on the slopes of a hill giving good views over a lake. Rivers and streams fed the lake, and one of the locations where the rocks could be found was on rising ground on its opposite side, and he was aware that there were good times and bad times for crossing the wetlands.

The effects of the last rainy season had passed and the grazing herds were on the move, the zebra foals still small but growing sturdier and keeping up with the adults. The air smelt dry, and the clear sky carried no threat of storms. All the signs told Kifimbo that the main river would be low enough to wade across if they went soon. Now was a good time.

The group he took included both experienced stone knappers and some older juveniles, and when they departed all carried pieces of hide and animal horns, and the strong staves which went everywhere with them.

Once across the river, the group turned along the flank of the hill, scanning for landmarks remembered from previous visits. Tough little shrubs and vines often obscured the outlines, but visual memories had been enhanced by the adhesiveness of spoken language. Images arrived in the mind inseparable from their relevant acoustic labels - words and phrases - and these helped to locate significant features.

"Big rock-fall. Near river bend."

Kifimbo was pointing ahead, knowing that just up from a jumble of massive boulders was the seam they'd been looking for.

Now they began to check out the immediate area for animal signs, and see if the rock shelter used previously would still serve for the period they'd be here. The air was filled with the sound of their voices, calling out and confirming that the rocky overhang that would protect their backs hadn't been claimed as a hyena den.

They rested while the sun was hot, then set about collecting caterpillars, insects and leaves to add to the shoots they'd plucked from the margins of the river bed as they'd made their way across.

After they'd eaten, the group spread out along the seam, but for Kifimbo the first task was to direct the juveniles who were uncertain about what to do. Instructions were essential, or in their ignorance the youngsters would have simply crowded round the first man to begin prising cores out of the layers exposed in the outcrop, or gone off to hack willy-nilly at unsuitable deposits.So Kifimbo led them away from the rock face to where they could get a better view of the seam.

"You with Nuru," he said, gesturing a youngster to go and learn from one of the older men.

"Pili watch there," he pointed, selecting another to be the look-out.

"Badru with me," to another.

~~~~~~~~
~~~~~~~~

Verbal instruction had probably grown out of the self-commentary of earlier times. Tasks were often accompanied by words and phrases, and children's spontaneous imitation of this feature would support their own learning of the tasks they observed. For the young, learning by watching did, of course, have its parallels in other species: leopard cubs shadowed their mother, adopting the stealthy approach to selected prey. Then they in their turn would provide a model for their own offspring. For the young of late Ergaster hominins, however, spoken language facilitated the whole process, accelerating progress towards competence, continuing its fundamental role of enabling them to survive.

Words weren't just helpful specific labels, though. They reflected the expansion and organisation that had been going on in the brain. There were the advances in how stone was being selected and used – the processes of observation and evaluation, then the physical manipulation to create a desired shape - and the tendency for the right hand to be used differently from the left. Such activities influenced how the brain was developing.[2] Add to all this a degree of verbal expression, and the formation of concepts was a possibility. When someone understood the meaning of a word, instant connections could be made to associated realms of knowledge, gathered through experience. Things could be thought about.

~~~~~~~~

The group talked as they worked, their voices echoing back and forth over the sound of cracking rocks and the rattle of stones dislodged. Overhead
~~~~~~~~

a pair of fish eagles added their own duet, calling and answering, focused on the river below. To them the hominins were just part of the background scenery.

Even the river itself contributed to the clan's haul. Rounded pebbles had piled into mounds beyond a point where two promontories came close, swept along and worn smooth when the water roared through. These would act as hammer-stones and missiles, and the youths collected them, needing no expertise other than the feel of a stone's contours sitting easily in the palm of the hand, or its lethal weight.

In the evening Kifimbo began a low pleased crooning with the fading of the light. The group had clustered under the overhang, and automatically the other men and youngsters took up the simple harmonious chant. The curve of the roof amplified it, throwing the sound around in ways that were yet another novel experience for the young, and the sensation kept them intrigued and singing until tiredness overcame them and they finally slept.

Next morning they began examining more closely the large, crude cores they had amassed, to discard flawed stone and begin working the best. Squatting on a flattish piece of ground not far from the quarry, the group set to, with juveniles gradually honing their skills. Whilst experienced knappers might talk among themselves, the young needed to focus all their concentration. The process of flaking didn't lend itself readily to explanations or instructions, so if anything was said it was more likely to have been 'Show me'. In time there would be a *feeling* for when a core had been well-struck, and visual satisfaction at a tear-shape achieved. Maybe practical help played a part, such as a guiding hand, but it was probably observation and aptitude, plus practice, which yielded success.[3]

~~~~~~~~

When the members of Kifimbo's clan left the site to return to their hillside base, the litter from their activity remained: unused inferior rock, struck flakes, spoiled tools. The evidence of their industry lay amongst that of previous generations, and those who came after would deposit yet more: thousands of pieces of debris, all in the same location, unearthed by palaeoarchaeologists nearly a million years later and telling the story of countless similar expeditions – of a group of people engaged together for a common purpose.[4]

To make such a trek to the outcrop, Kifimbo may have drawn on the extra organising ability that language was contributing to the workings of his mind. But elephants visited certain waterholes at particular times, excavating the surrounding mud for essential salts when they felt a need for them, so Kifimbo's expedition was no different in many respects from that. What set it apart, however, was that the task required a cooperative effort from a mixture of individuals whose experience and know-how varied. He might have initiated the expedition, or negotiated the timing of it, maybe decided on variations to the route to be followed, and this was a sort of planning – telling the group what would need to be done. Perhaps it had its roots in the old vocal displays of the dominant male, imposing his authority on his subordinates, but it had expanded and refined itself. Such a diversity of expression drew on the connections that went to all the major sensory lobes of his cortex – to Kifimbo's
~~~~~~~~

recollection of everything that had been seen, heard and done on previous expeditions, and to his understanding of how his people might respond.

Interacting in this way was probably a natural progression from the games of a long childhood and the testing grounds of early manhood. Words could deal with the details of situations, and phrases could manipulate others – thereby, hopefully, repeating successful outcomes.

Maybe too the process was instrumental in the formation of a clan, and in the dynamics of its hierarchy. A prospective leader, with just a little more insight into how a situation should be handled would use verbal skills to manage ventures, and motivate individuals to work together towards a common goal. That goal however could easily be out of sight and out of mind to some individuals, so the language of leadership would be the key to enabling larger groups to capitalise on their strength of numbers.

Even so, what spoken language these people used may well have been quite basic in style – sequences of brief utterances maybe no more than one, two or three words in length, and it would be tempting to think of them as inadequate to the task of organising a workforce. Yet present-day infants between two and three years old are perfectly capable of using such limited self-expression to great effect. Eavesdrop on the negotiations which take place between children and their carers in the aisles of supermarkets, try to get out of playing favourite games over and over, or to curtail a bedtime story (or to go to bed in the first place), and the persuasive power of basic language speaks for itself.

Kifimbo may well have been persuading people to cooperate in regular working parties at Olorgesailie, but the site also reveals the drama of a particular event in late *Homo ergaster* life, with its hints at other kinds of behaviour and the kind of communication that might have gone with it.

The hillside camp overlooking the lake continued to be used on and off during many fluctuations of climate. Sometimes, when the level of water dropped to the point where vegetation took over its bed, the late Ergaster people would have had to move away onto the dry grasslands to find prey. Before that however, at times when the Olorgesailie basin became a marshy wetland, animals that came to graze among the reeds could be watched, and targeted. It is evident that descendants of Kifimbo's clan could even take on elephants – the huge predecessors of those living today.

What kind of strategy did they adopt to stalk and bring down such a creature? Surely one that involved members of a hunting band coordinating different roles – distracting, wounding, overpowering, killing. It's hard to imagine that some verbal rehearsing of possible approaches wouldn't have taken place prior to the attack.

However it was achieved, down by the marsh the clan slaughtered and butchered an elephant. They brought unworked cores to the site, and struck sharp flakes from them there and then.

When the fossilised bones were excavated, cut marks could be seen on the ribs, vertebrae and even the hyoid bone – where the muscles of the tongue had been attached. More than two thousand stone artefacts surrounded the remains of the carcase. Not far away more butchered bones provide evidence of late Ergaster people eating the meat of zebra and antelope.

The hunters had had the confidence to stay where they were for long enough to deal with large carcases; the vultures and hyenas, big cats and giant baboons could, it seems, be kept at bay – at least for a while. And when all was done, the clanspeople retreated uphill to their base and ate in safety – and maybe they built a narrative in phrases that described the extraordinary events of the day. Seeds, nuts, berries, roots and tubers were the staple diet, so meat was an occasional, very special bounty. Letting go of the fear, excitement, danger and success of the hunt through venting their feelings in words would give opportunities not just to relive the experience, but to record it, to demonstrate prowess, and to elevate status.

Sitting along with the adults as the meat was shared out (or competed for) the children too would have been participants in these social dynamics. They would have used their listening skills to try to understand the accounts of what had happened (an event they may have watched...) but they would probably also have had little difficulty in sensing what else was going on under the surface. However valuable verbal communication was becoming in its practical application to the late Ergaster way of life, one of its most fundamental functions was still concerned with relationships – who was dominant, who could be trusted, who was conciliatory, who would give help when it was needed.

And the roots of that aspect of spoken language lay, as ever, in infancy. Helpless late Ergaster infants were just as desperate to secure the care and attention of their closest kin as previous disadvantaged young hominins. Maybe they were even more desperate; if hunting proficiency meant that meat played a bigger role in the diet, infant dependency actually increased. Once weaned they might forage, but they couldn't hunt for themselves, so the best they could hope for was that family members would cut some of the meat up into suitably small portions, and give it to them. Fostering helpful bonds in a widening social circle was vital: communication was under pressure again.

<u>The seedbed for spoken language...</u>

- From an early age, the infants of late Ergaster groups were highly motivated to use their communication skills to create positive bonds within an enlarging social circle.

- Within bigger peer groups, infant hominins had greater need to develop vocabulary and find verbal ways of influencing how others behaved towards them.

- Adult activities exposed infants to how cooperation occurred, fostering a sense of the future and the beginnings of planning – both of which might be conveyed verbally.

- The gap between infant and adult language was now wider, so another element emerged in the interplay between infants and their care-givers: listening to expressions of intention and re-telling of exploits allowed infants to hear and understand verbal language in a more connected style, helping to establish longer auditory memory. This would be an essential prerequisite for their own longer utterances.

CHAPTER 11

Children with Questions

Homo heidelbergensis…300,000 years ago

The ability to hunt elephants may have kept late Ergaster families going for some time, but for those populations who had migrated north, leaving Africa along the eastern Mediterranean, prey species came in smaller sizes, and they moved faster. Tactics would have to change again.

By about 500,000 years ago, the migrants into Europe had indeed adapted, and the subtle alterations detected in their anatomy have led them to be classified as another species on the human family tree: *Homo heidelbergensis*. They weren't as robust as Ergaster, but their brain size, at 1200cc was slightly bigger – they were having to use their wits again, and those who were successful could venture even further into new landscapes. By 300,000 years ago, among other places, they were living in Spain.

~~~~~~~~

Nyuni began to feel bored with tossing pebbles into the river. He'd followed the track down from the wide ledge outside his family's cave shelter, scrambling ahead of his parents and little brother, and amusing himself by seeing how big a splash he could make.

Now he glanced along the bank to where his mother had joined a few other women gathering rushes, and a sense of uncertainty and apprehension came back to him. Normally the air
~~~~~~~~

would have been filled with the sound of voices, but their talk was muted; the group smaller than it used to be.

His father too had been subdued, but that had been easier for Nyuni to cope with than the raging he'd witnessed recently. What had made it worse was the terrible commotion everywhere – days when men were yelling and shouting, and the women wailing. He'd approached his mother, tight-shouldered and with a timid "What, what?" question, but she'd ignored him, rocking back and forth with her eyes closed, tears coursing down her face.

Their daily need for food had forced the family back into routine, so that although the atmosphere was volatile, activity made it less troubling – except that Nyuni felt something very bad had happened.

He ran to catch up with Tumbo, his small brother, who had been trailing along behind their mother, and together they watched as the women pulled at the rushes. These had to be slapped on flat rocks in the river in order to rid them of silt, and it was the splashing of water and the wet thwack of the stems that captured Tumbo's attention. Nyuni tried to hear what the women were saying but for Tumbo, their talk went right over his head.

Capriciously, having been grounded in the overwhelming impotence of infants, spoken language seemed now to be aligning itself more and more with the concerns and behaviour of adults. Were infants really letting the initiative go, relinquishing their creative role?

Certainly, it wouldn't be obvious if they were still the driving force, given the widening gap between what adults were using language for, and what infants did with it. But infants still had to ensure care-givers would attend to them, and increasingly the reaction of older kin was to encourage speech, on much the same basis as they helped children tackle new foods – it came naturally.

As soon as the small boy pushed in beside them, the women adjusted the way they talked. For his safety he would have to stay nearby, so they needed to keep him interested in what they were doing; it was the human version of the tactics used by other animals to ensure the young didn't stray – a light thwack with a paw, 'shepherding' between adults as elephants did, or a specific, directed call. As for Nyuni, he knew the chance of finding anything out by eavesdropping was gone now, and he soon left them all to it, wandering away in search of a playmate.

The women quickly involved Tumbo in the activity.

"This good rush!" said one, loudly. "Pull hard, pull *hard,*" she instructed, and Tumbo added his groans to hers as they dramatised.

The little boy's mother said "Tumbo carry rushes, carry rushes," and the words came out deliberately, and she paused before telling him what to do next. She talked as they worked, and all the while her voice had bigger changes of pitch than when she spoke to Nyuni, heightening the emphasis to keep Tumbo listening.[1] For it was the case that small children didn't have a problem with watching what caught their attention – they could become fascinated by what they saw adults and older children doing – but that was only till something else came along.

Listening to spoken language was, in evolutionary terms, a new skill, and Tumbo would have been easily distracted. Instinctively he would have turned at the movement of an animal, the cry of a bird of prey, and any unknown sound could alarm him. To be sure, the newer skill had determined that, as a baby, he had babbled when he heard human voices, playing with what his own lips and tongue could do, and he'd focused intently on his mother's face and voice, listening and learning all the while he was near her. But once he was walking and greedy to find out about his surroundings, he was in an adult-orientated world, humming with adult communication and it wasn't easy to concentrate on these human strings of sound.Like the problems infants encountered in dealing with the food that adults ate – needing it broken down - the same was true of spoken language: it was essential, and the more complicated it became the more it had to be prepared, made easy for them to digest.[2]

~~~~~~~~

Neither process involved foresight, though. Food satisfied an immediate hunger; the fact that it enabled a small infant to grow to adult stature was a fortunate consequence. In the case of spoken language too, the techniques that the women and any care-giver used with infants were automatic moment-by-moment interactions that had developed to provide the right "nourishment". Perhaps it was the case that all they were really doing was letting their communication slip back to their own excited, earlier styles, stimulated by the presence of someone younger.

Whatever the underlying mechanism, the outcome would certainly be growth, but mature language wasn't a deliberate objective. Even today
~~~~~~~~

the habit of using simpler speech, with repeated words and phrases and varying vocal pitch seems a universal one, and although we realise now how much it helps children develop their language, the impulse is driven by instinct, not knowledge. Is it possible that, as a species, we too find it easy to slip back, because spoken language in us remained at this kind of level for hundreds of thousands of years – a simple style, deeply ingrained...?

Another aspect of the process was that the women talked about routines, and this was very much to Tumbo's advantage; out of context the expressions they used would have had very limited value to him. With the inevitable repetitions, however, he gradually understood what he heard – because he saw the meaning demonstrated day by day. Often Tumbo echoed what someone said, and they responded, saying it back, and that really did help him to learn.

~~~~~~~~

Tumbo soon began splashing in the shallows, but suddenly noticed that further along one of the older men was standing on the bank hacking away at the stem of a shrub. The large stone he was using had been flaked on both sides so was both sharp and heavy. With the slender branch sliced off he stood back, obviously selecting another stem for the same treatment.

"Hurani do..?" said Tumbo.

He paddled to his mother, patting her thigh and pointing.

"Yeh?" she nodded, "yeh."

He pulled at her hand. "See Hurani!"
~~~~~~~~

Leaving the pile of reeds, the woman went with Tumbo, his interest obviously having taken off and gone elsewhere; he would only be safe if accompanied and his inquisitiveness satisfied.[3] Apart from that, his brain was most receptive to what he himself was focussed on, so he'd remember better whatever followed next.

Hurani now had three straight stems on the ground in front of him, each one a little thicker than Tumbo's arm, and he squatted on his haunches, scrutinising his assortment of tools. He looked up as he heard Tumbo's enquiring voice.

"What do?"

The man smiled. He took one of the finest of his flakes, and then with swift downward strokes stripped it of twigs; next he angled the flake towards one end of the branch, rapidly producing a fine point as he turned it in his hand.

"Make spear," he said.

Tumbo frowned, and Hurani play-acted what he would do with the spear, accompanying his performance with phrases simple enough for Tumbo to comprehend. Tumbo's mother said "for meat" and an image came to him of the carcases he saw being butchered – from the animals Hurani had killed with a spear.[4]

"Do again," said Tumbo, pointing at the branches and he stood engrossed as Hurani went through the craft of making spears, more slowly this time, and reflecting again through his words how they would be used. Tumbo's mother went back to the stream, and the child stayed to watch and listen. When Hurani had finished, the child squatted to pick up the flakes from his hand axe.

"No!"

Tumbo drew back, looking up at the man's face.

"Sharp, hurt you." The frowning expression, the urgency in Hurani's voice, his intonation – this stopped Tumbo, then he understood the words.

He waited while Hurani gathered everything together, still watching.

"Tumbo come Hurani," said the man.

"What do now?" The question spilled out.

~~~~~~~~

There had, in hominin vocalisations, always been an available intonation pattern for conveying uncertainty – a rising note – and a suitable facial expression to go with it. But young and demanding infants had forced a liaison between this and a few particular sounds to form the words 'what', or 'where' or 'who' - to make the question specific; that way they might get at the answer they wanted.[5] It was their agenda - the priority for infants was finding things out, because the big brain continued to be a mixed blessing and the young took ever longer to mature. Asking questions was an inspired short cut to amassing knowledge, and like other innovations, it was a habit that would certainly stick.

The answers were something else again, of course, and if speech was to fulfil its function for infants at all, it had to transmit its meaning like an urgent coded message – as quickly as it could, because the young had another disadvantage. They had a short attention span, were easily distracted, and it was their short-term memory that would rush to store what was said if it was ever to be absorbed for their own use. So the sounds had to come as fast as Heidelbergensis breath, voice, lips and tongue could coordinate them, with every syllable laden with information. This may not have
~~~~~~~~

been high speed, intricate stuff, however. For the Heidelbergensis people there were components that had yet to be fully exploited, a particular evolutionary contribution that had to come into its own before spoken language could really take off.

Nevertheless to achieve that vital understanding, even this level of verbal communication had capitalised on an inherent acuity of hearing, by which the contrast in the frequencies of sounds could signal important differences in meaning – a feature which would have appeared in the earliest syllables an infant might understand. For example, in distinguishing "Papa" from "Mama" only the momentary buzz of the voice caused "m" to differ from "p" – being identically made by the lips. And as for "nose" and "toes", the clue was the nasal buzz at the start of one and the quiet plosive tap at the start of the other – nothing was visible.

Fortunately for the young, having had this facility at their disposal from so early on, it was already up and running as their experiences widened; gradually too they found it easier to listen for longer. Spoken language could therefore safely expand into phrases because these structures still allowed meaning to remain tightly compressed. By rearranging sounds, recombining syllables, and ordering units in particular ways, linguistic communication could develop flexibly and still retain its economy. But it was thanks entirely to infants that it emerged in the way it did, because it was *their* learning style that dictated it – the design fitted in with the way immature brains worked, not adult ones.

The 'design' itself - the way words and phrases might take shape – probably owed much to the physiological systems which had given rise to vocal communication in the first place: nerves grew and branched, so did the circulatory system supplying the muscles. They functioned by way of an efficient pattern, and in its growth, maybe language behaved almost like an extension of it.

~~~~~~~~

Hurani led the little boy back to the women, who were now moving away from the river, starting to climb back up to the caves. His conversation with Tumbo had been typically brief – just meeting his need for information. Until children were old enough to talk in roughly the same style as adults, older kin weren't especially prone to start conversations with them, even if they did modify their speech when responding.[6] There were usually children of varying ages around who played and chattered and shared each other's interests, accompanying what they did with speech at whatever level they'd reached.

So Tumbo looked around for Nyuni, needing his brother again. He saw that he was back by the riverside, sitting disconsolately, insecure for the first time in his life.

Since some while ago – he had no idea how long - Nyuni hadn't seen several of his kinsfolk – some older cousins, their mates, a girl playmate of his own age and her father and mother. A mixed group like this occasionally went off together if a good supply of berries had been found or a herd of horses spotted, but they always came back – at least most of them did. Juveniles (youngsters between about nine and twelve) were often reckless and might fall victim to wild animals. But Nyuni knew somehow that none of his missing
~~~~~~~~

family members was going to return, and he didn't understand and it was frightening.

Then Tumbo shouted, jerking him out of his preoccupation, and he got to his feet and joined the little group trailing up to the cave ledge, noticing on the way that Hurani had gone up too, getting ahead of the women and branching off along a track leading onto the plateau. Suddenly interested, Nyuni went after him.

The area was a rough, boulder-strewn wilderness, and Hurani had picked his way to where the ground levelled in front of a tumble of rocks and straggly trees. Hurani turned as Nyuni came up beside him, studying him for a moment, then pointed at an opening between the rocks.

"They down there," he said.

Nyuni peered into the gap. Other cracks and gaps let light in, and when his eyes had adjusted, Nyuni could see that this wasn't a normal cave, but a wide shaft, and very deep. At the bottom were the bodies, lying together where they'd been thrown. They weren't moving. They were all dead.

The boy had accepted single deaths from time to time, but this was too many – and they were people to whom he belonged.

He stared, and as the realisation of what he was seeing hit him, began to sob.

"They stink," said Hurani.

It was true, and the smell would have drawn vultures and carnivores had such a large group been left out in the open near their base. But all Nyuni felt was loss and fear.

Had he been able to ask *why* so many kin were dead down there together, and to concentrate long enough on a spoken explanation to absorb it, he would have heard that the foraging expedition had gone some distance without finding anything substantial to bring back. This could often be the case – there were periods when malnourishment was a normal state of affairs – and so the group had had to resort to scavenging off a large bird carcase. How it had died was impossible to tell, and if it had been diseased, that would explain why within hours of eating, each of the group suffered violent fevers, and in days, all had died. The shaft was a solution to the problem of the bodies.

But Hurani had adult spoken language that was direct, grounded in the moment – and though it was able to express intention, or relate a past event, it wasn't capable of working through a sequence of several events and offering possible reasons. So he couldn't have explained why he'd been drawn to go back to the place – perhaps it was just some sort of contact with his kin.

He sighed, turning away from the rocky outcrop, and gestured to Nyuni; together they went down from the plateau.

Nyuni was distracted by the experience for days; the image of his dead kinsfolk kept coming back and he remained troubled. His mother watched out for him more than usual - he wasn't alert to opportunities for enjoyment, and she could tell that this affected his general well-being. His senses were dulled, so he was more vulnerable than ever.

~~~~~~~~

Such a situation as the loss of a whole section of his community would unsettle any youngster in a socially functioning species. We expect small children to get upset when their parents leave them
~~~~~~~~

at Nursery for the first few times, and know that there'll be tears after loved visitors have left to go home. The death of a close family member is particularly problematic. While they're very little, hugs and cuddles provide comfort, but as they grow older we can try to explain things: "Mummy'll be back soon", "Uncle Peter's gone on a plane, but he'll come and see us again at Christmas", "Grannie was very old, and her legs hurt her a lot, and she was very tired. We won't see her any more, but she still loves us." It's not easy, but as children's capacity for understanding grows we can increasingly use spoken language to console them.

For the Heidelbergensis adults at Atapuerca 300,000 years ago, even though emotionally affected, the imperative of finding food and staying safe would force them to focus the mind elsewhere – there would be more to do now there were fewer family members around. Infants were in a different position – bewildered and frightened - and it might have been they who most needed ways to regain their feelings of normality. Like little Tumbo, perhaps they asked questions, but they were probably those of the simplest kind: "what?", and "who?" and "where?" – questions grounded in the familiar, in something demonstrable, like the shaping of a spear. It might be a long time before spoken language had the wherewithal to formulate "why?", because the answer could involve delving into the mind's images, turning over alternatives, and that's a speculation too far. As for the Atapuerca site itself, questions are still being asked about what caused the deaths of the thirty-two individuals discovered there during excavations in the 1980's. A fatal infection *may* have been the explanation, but there are other possibilities, of course. It is a place that has become known as 'The Pit of Bones' – and both the name and the thought of what might have taken place there makes us shudder a little, in spite of ourselves.

So even we can't explain, and however far the Heidelbergensis people got with their language,[7] it would be another human species much closer in time to ourselves whose lifestyle suggests an even bigger role for verbal communication.

<u>The seedbed for spoken language...</u>
- A hunter-gatherer lifestyle demanded a variety of skills: heidelbergensis infants increased their vocabulary by watching and listening to adults as they went about their daily tasks.
- Care-givers instinctively responded to their limited attention span, capturing or following their interests, communicating in ways that worked at their level.
- The interdependency of small heidelbergensis groups strengthened the emotional bonds within them. Infants were particularly affected by these, and spoken language would be under pressure to accommodate to this aspect of human experience.
- Specific issues that concerned them would prompt children to develop and use verbal questions.

CHAPTER 12

A Social Life

The animals were large, both sexes having horns almost as long as a man's arm, and the males distinctive by reason of dewlaps. They could cover great distances, jumping spectacularly when alarmed, and it was this which Hiba had seen out of the corner of her eye as she scoured a rocky outcrop looking for seed-heads. Dropping quickly back, and with a high-pitched call, she brought her companions alongside and for a while they observed the small herd as it resumed feeding.

There were perhaps thirty or so animals of mixed ages, and as they neared the rougher terrain associated with the river, it became clear that the elands' likely route would bring them close to where a steep cliff rose above a wide, flat bank.

Gesturing, and with urgent whispers, the adults in the twenty-strong band sorted out a strategy. Forcing a stampede which would drive the eland over the cliff had been attempted before.[1] It was straightforward in principle, but succeeded only rarely in practice. They waited, poised.

When the drive commenced, the children and Hiba, positioned on the rocky outcrop could see everything. Hearts thumping, they struggled to keep silent as the hunters erupted from cover, yelling and leaping, running the animals through the scrub and rocks so that the entire herd took off in panic – heading in the only direction possible: the cliff.

In dust and silence it was all over.

Scrambling down onto the grassy bank the group surveyed their kill. The eland were piled one on top of the other, old, young, and those in their prime: a heap of bodies. The amount of meat they represented was prodigious. Help would be necessary to bring the carcases back to the cave, and in any case, there was more than enough to go round - such abundance had got to be shared.

It wasn't long before two of the juveniles – fast runners – set off towards another clan's home base. They had listened intently to the hunters' message, saying the instruction over and over to fix it in their minds. Retaining the contents of lengthier utterances had proved invaluable as cooperative tasks had multiplied – and the necessity of doing this had ensured that attending to speech, having focused on it right from earliest infancy, had become deeply ingrained. Speech was getting much better at conveying any proposed plan of action.

As soon as it had been received by the neighbouring group, the message would be passed on and acted on. Over the following few days, many people from the surrounding area would be making their way to the Klasies River Mouth Cave - extended families joining together in one of the most enjoyable spin-offs of cooperation.

~~~~~~~~

Once more, the setting for the on-going story of spoken language was the continent of Africa.

During the millennia that had passed since *Homo heidelbergensis*, long ice ages had come and gone, severe and far-reaching, and in their intensity they had taken the human population of
~~~~~~~~

Africa to the very limits of existence. Forced to seek refuge wherever plant and animal life was holding on, viable communities which had overcome the hardships were few and far between.

Some had made their way down the continent, and because warmth could return quickly, a small group of clans had settled here on the southern coast. The ocean currents would keep the temperature a little higher, and their skills and adaptations would prove enough to keep them going.

By 90,000 years ago, these people now had the lithe limbs associated with living in hotter climates. They had distinct eyebrows rather than a continuous ridge, and the big brain, with its impressive 1350cc volume, had expanded in regions which changed the shape of the skull. The face was flat, except for a projecting chin, and it was tucked in beneath a vertical forehead; these were early modern people – their species was *Homo sapiens*.

~~~~~~~~

Sometimes the group which occupied the Klasies River Mouth cave would loosely follow the river's course back to spend time within easy reach of the open scrub. It provided the seeds and berries, insects, leaves and underground tubers which still formed a staple part of the diet. In addition the area's game animals were varied and abundant.

The cave wasn't necessarily a permanent base - the group had access to enough territory to roam if need be - so when a particular bounty came their way, as on this occasion, it was simply a case of
~~~~~~~~

being in the right place at the right time that gave them the opportunity to take the eland.

Now, Hiba's task was to call the children together and return with the news to her own family who had remained at the River Mouth cave. These were two female relatives with very young infants, a few older males and two elderly women; these in particular would welcome the variety of company and the renewing of friendships which the event heralded.

One of them, Hiba's mother, was down on the seashore on the lookout for anything edible that the tide had brought in, but she abandoned the search as soon as she heard the noise from above. Later, she and some of the children would scour the surrounding area, beach and headlands alike, collecting wood to feed the fires, because the meat would be cooked.

~~~~~~~~

The taming of fire had probably begun about 400,000 years before – another example of the sort of stunt a big brain might pull off.[2] And it had certainly proved worth taking the obvious risks. During the long periods of cold, being able to keep warm had no doubt played a major part in whether or not a whole community survived, never mind an individual.

Also, if fire had made life easier during the harsh years of wandering, it had been making eating easier too. Prepared by cooking, meat could be introduced much sooner to the young, with obvious benefits, and the innovation kept grandmothers alive, allowing them to eat when elderly teeth and jaws might have baulked at raw food as in times
~~~~~~~~

past. This was another bonus. Relieved of reproductive burdens, grandmothers fetched food when the mothers and new-born of family groups needed to stay sheltered from the elements, they were available caregivers in general, and with up to thirty-five years of life's experiences behind them, they were the valued holders of memories.[3]

When they passed on their wisdom, those who listened stretched their own retentive powers; it was important to capture knowledge and keep it. Repetition helped, and children, who were the experts, learnt very early on how to extend their ability to recall what had been said, until, of course, they fell asleep.

~~~~~~~~

Naturally, fire had other features to its credit. Discouraging the attention of hungry predators was certainly one, but what about the social comfort its warmth and flickering light invited? Such an asset was here to stay, and now these early modern people would gather round a hearth on open ground if the evenings were safe and warm, or light their fire inside the cave if there was something prowling, or the sea roared and spat in the teeth of a gale.

With families converging because of the eland drive there would need to be fuel for more fires, and enough to last several days. People may have travelled some way, and the chance for socialising was extremely precious.

~~~~~~~~

What kind of spoken language would they have been using, though?

In all of Africa, the evidence from genetic studies suggests that between 100,000 and 50,000 years ago the adversities of the preceding millennia had reduced the peoples' numbers to maybe no more than 10,000 adults. So had these pressures induced further development in how they communicated with each other? Did a talent for talking make a contribution to their survival? Using up energy competing with each other for resources would hardly have made any sense in environments where humans were also competing with the rest of the animal kingdom. On the other hand, the ability to join forces and a willingness to share know-how may have been about the only attribute they had in their favour.

Events affecting human circumstances had repeatedly been the stimuli for both anatomical and behavioural adaptations, and if a relentlessly dwindling population wasn't a challenge for the species, then what was? So having played a part thus far, it would be decidedly odd if the existing communication system hadn't cast about for new ways of operating, as people came to the brink. The rigours were endured by everyone, and infants weren't somehow cocooned; so if the family as a unit was under stress then they were too. The young, however, were the ones with the greatest neural adaptability. In them the response to pressure might have acted as the tinder which a small, helpful spark would set alight.

And that spark was possibly FOXP2.[4]

FOXP2 is a benign genetic mutation which has the power to influence other genes – including those in the brain. It occurs in other animals, but in us it is relevant to the development of certain aspects of motor co-ordination, enhancing the

muscular agility of the lower face and lips –
something which might produce a more dazzling
smile or pronounced pout. But if this was all it did,
natural selection could be forgiven for giving it just
a passing nod.

Instead it appears to have done much more.
Although rare, there are people today who lack this
genetic modification and whose speech and
language are impaired as a result. They find it hard
to coordinate the fast and complicated sequences
of movement which the mouth and face must make
if speech is to flow as expected, and they have
trouble using and understanding the subtleties of
language which are conveyed by grammar.

Whenever FOXP2 came to prominence in the
human species (and there is uncertainty about
when that was) there must have been a system
already established which would be receptive to
improvements as useful as greater oral agility. If
there was nothing much for it to work on, why would
it spread throughout the human population?

But spread it did, and it had plenty of time, if, as
is thought, the crucial differences in FOXP2
appeared about 200,000 years ago. Suppose
communication had indeed developed in the way
described in this story, then by 90,000 years ago
many benefits could have accumulated.

Spoken language, having already gone beyond
the body language and non-verbal signals with
which it co-existed, would have been doing its best,
but could only develop so far. Physical capacities
determined what was achievable in the actual
production of speech, setting limits. This mutation
could throw a switch, however, and facilitate faster,
more precise movement. By the time fully modern
people – ourselves - had exploited its benefits,

something extraordinary had happened. Today we're unable to process information that is visual, or sounds that aren't speech sounds, any faster than 7 – 9 items per second. Speech, however, is in a class of its own. It is transmitted at a staggering15 – 25 sounds per second,[5] and for each and every one of those sounds precise coordination and control comes without thinking. We understand it at that speed too.

With the arrival of FOXP2 (and any other similarly helpful genetic mutation yet to be identified) spoken language would be on its way to this kind of performance. New sounds could emerge out of finer neuromuscular control, because it only took the smallest of changes in shape of lips or placement of tongue to add another variation to the repertoire. And *more* sounds increased the options for combining sounds, so there'd be greater scope for reflecting shades of meaning through speech. Some consonants could be articulated much more closely together – not needing to fit a vowel in between – because the muscles could make the slide from one consonant to the next swiftly and seamlessly.[6] And phrases could run into one another, connected speech could flow. If speech had been laboured and slow before, now it could accelerate. If it had been staccato and halting before – brief discrete elements embedded within a call - now it was streamlining itself.[7] In other words, a lot more could be said in the same amount of time.

Obligingly, and more importantly, the mutation took on the consequences of its own improvements; it would also be involved in processing connected speech, helping people understand what was being said – necessarily growing in tandem if spoken language was now emerging as a more rapid and concentrated mix of auditory data.

And Hiba's forbears would have possessed FOXP2. Genetic studies have shown that there was a woman living in Africa about 150,000 years ago whose make-up would have included the mutation, and with whom every person in the world today shares his or her ancestry.[8] It's believed she came from north-east Africa, perhaps Kenya or Ethiopia. Her descendants dispersed, and wherever they went they took fire, the cognitive skills to cope with the effects of climate change on their habitats, a supportive social structure - and the genetic asset that would prompt the use and understanding of more nimble, nuanced spoken language.

Faster, denser acoustic data could more easily convey details about individual experiences, making them available for perusal by everyone; if there was something to be gained by another's success or failure, the whole community benefited; an eland hunt might be repeated if techniques could be described to those who weren't there.

~~~~~~~~

It wasn't all talk around the fires, of course. The curling smoke and sparks crackling up into the night sky were adding their atmosphere to the old compulsion of beating a rhythm; the inclination to sing and dance was very near the surface on occasions like this.

Hiba, at fourteen, was aware that this gathering would present her with the chance of finding a mate, and there were in the two or three clans
~~~~~~~~

present several young men and girls at similar stages in their lives. By dint of her healthy appearance and pleasant nature Hiba was one of those who succeeded in attracting attention.

Kipanga sought her out the following day and made his interest obvious, appearing close by while she foraged, making her smile with his efforts to reach fruit from high branches, and stopping to rest when she did.

When his family group decided it was time to return to their territory, Kipanga stayed behind. He was a welcome extra pair of hands, and by the time Hiba became pregnant, the feast was just a good memory, and the members of her family group and clan were enjoying bounty of a different kind: fur seals. Sometimes pups were washed up on the shore so required no effort at all, but at low tide strong swimmers like Kipanga could reach the rocks where the adult seals basked; out of water these were lumbering creatures and offered both meals and hide to an adept hunter.

So Hiba was well fed, the baby safely delivered, and with her mother's help she was soon ready to resume the normal patterns of daily living – but she would do this with her mate's family. Kipanga would return to his clan now, taking its new members with him.

Both his and Hiba's groups were practicing the old balancing trick of positioning themselves along the margins of two habitats, and although Kipanga's people would come down to the sea for a few weeks, their preferred surroundings were in the grasslands, attractive by reason of the opportunity to catch steenbok and other small grazing animals. This is where the young mother would raise her child, away from close kin and with the help of strangers.

She felt both sadness and apprehension at leaving her mother and younger sister and the wider family in which she had grown up. Long dependency had resulted in close attachments – not just with a parent, but with the whole group of kin. And for those Hiba would leave behind, her departure represented a disruption too: they all needed one another in untold ways.

But early modern people were probably coping very much better with this sort of thing than the Heidelbergensis before them, thanks to the ways in which spoken language had been evolving.[9]

<p style="text-align:center">~~~~~~~~</p>

Right from its earliest origins in both the individual and the species, spoken language hadn't just been about vocabulary and information, command and enquiry; it had fulfilled a very social function as well. During the tough times, when the ramifications of climate change took their inexorable toll of a clan's vulnerable members, the need would be for the expression through speech of fears and feelings, and an approach to problems through more intense questioning. All these might have clarified the options open to a clan as its members sought to manage their plight. And although nothing would happen overnight, with the planting of FOXP2's microscopic seed of change, more wide-ranging verbal communication was there for the taking.

Over time, and exactly as their forebears had done, these early modern people had begun the process as infants, using their voices because there was nothing else available to make their

192

presence felt. Through childhood they had extracted everything they could from their accumulated neurological inheritance, playing with new sounds, finding amusement in the way syllables could form words. The sheer pleasure of talking did the groundwork for early modern infants, making it natural for them to use innovative ways to get feelings across and find combinations of phrases that worked just that bit better as interactions with care-givers and kin. It would be a short step to alter the order of words or tack on another sound, changing meanings just a little. They each took with them into adulthood a slightly newer version of spoken language – and the next generation did the same in its turn. Infants and children were predisposed to behave like that – not because effective spoken language would be really useful in the future, but because the legacy of the past gave children an irrepressible urge to talk.

When the climate relaxed again, so could the people, and the hints left at the Klasies River Mouth cave do suggest the early modern lifestyle was characterised by communal living of a different order from that which had gone before. The animal bones and charred ground that have been uncovered there were left by people who were beginning to exert more control over aspects of their existence; the immediate opportunity which had to be taken, and the creation of a particular context for social encounters. These might not wait for the outcome of a slow and cumbersome debate. If action were needed the chances are that it would take the concerted efforts of a sizeable number of people. A level of spoken language which efficiently spanned informative, social and emotional functions was vital – because people's willingness to collaborate owed much to how well they got on with each other.

The ice ages had inflicted almost unimaginable hardships on our ancient ancestors, but nature had equipped their infants with the potential to survive. And their solution hadn't been just about how to keep warm. It had driven another spurt of growth in spoken language.

<hr>

<u>The seedbed for spoken language…</u>
- Environmental hardships continued to put pressure on the individual from birth onwards. Any feature would be inclined to adapt if it conferred an advantage.
- The presence of FOXP2 would allow the physical enrichment of speech, and the processing of this more complex expressive language.
- The early modern lifestyle offered situations in which enhanced communication could be utilized to the full.
- More adept communication, having a wide range of functions, would contribute to both an individual and a population's wellbeing – just the kind of conditions likely to establish and prompt the spread of the genetic components involved.

<hr>

CHAPTER 13

Fitting In

Early Modern People…90,000 years ago – continued.

Hiba's primary task, if her baby was to grow to womanhood, would be to make positive relationships with Kipanga's extended family, though she had no inkling that the one had implications for the other. Hiba just reacted to her new situation as best she could. It helped that a female cousin was already there, but Hiba took care to recognise for herself who was who in the scheme of things. Her contribution was going to have emotional as well as practical effects and if she fitted in well that would rub off on the baby. The passing round and inspection of the baby duly took place at the start, but in the general activities of each day Hiba either carried or kept the infant close to her until she began to crawl, and then anyone would pick her up to calm and comfort her. It was assumed that the baby would feel secure with them, but this would only happen if Hiba felt at ease too. How she approached everyone demanded a blend of social skills old and new - or at least, old and less old. Accepted practices had accumulated over a vast time-span, and attitude would now be as evident from spoken language as it was from the body language which had preceded it; so asleep or awake, against her mother's skin, Hiba's baby absorbed a range of delicate nuances with all her senses.[1]

As for Kipanga's family, understanding an infant's cries – whether they were pain or hunger or frustration - was second nature to almost all of them, particularly those who were only just out of infancy themselves, and it was the children surrounding the baby as they played or accompanied their mothers who were often her care-givers. For the baby's part, she'd soon gained control of her eye movements, focusing intently on Hiba's face, and even before she was learning to sit up she had tuned in to the lively contours of their speech, as well as to Hiba's more familiar voice.[2] Under the shade of a gum tree, only the drone of insects or the rustle of leaves in the breeze competed, and unless a more primal stimulus distracted, speech was the most interesting noise around – and that included the sounds she made herself for her own pleasure and amusement. She could play with their rhythm and melody, and change the tone of her voice.[3] This was a vital time; once she was fully mobile, like Tumbo generations before, the objects of her curiosity would compete for her attention.

She was an out-going baby, though, and before she was a year old she could understand and imitate some gestures, such as those used in everyday greetings, and was vocalising and using signals to get what she wanted. As for words, she'd look towards Kipanga if her mother called to him, and when the children played, she'd turn to whoever was named, even though the game couldn't yet include herself.

More than any of the ancestral species before her, Hiba's baby's ability to understand speech would owe a great deal to what those ancestral species had grown used to hearing. Each cycle of climate change, each successive habitat presented vital information carried on the air, picked up and understood by the ear: the way a whirlwind warned of its approach, the crescendo of raindrops at the start of a storm, the silence afterwards. There was the sound a herd might make as it migrated, or the thunder of hooves when it fled from a predator, and the barely perceptible whisper of grass when an animal was on the prowl. Understanding what the environment said about itself was key to being able to stay alive in it – and early modern people would have that ability ingrained. Listening skills had literally come a long way since the Afarensis had left the enclosed gallery of the forest, and without an ability to discriminate between the smallest of sound frequencies and to appreciate their significance, human speech would have had no use for FOXP2. But the two features partnered each other, and speech could contain clicks and rasps, plosives and fricatives, sounds squeezed out laterally by the tongue, or with it curled back on itself, and the voice could be guttural or nasalised or it could change its tone – so long as auditory acuity was up to the job.

If she survived the first year Kipanga's family would give a name to Hiba's baby. But it would probably be *Mako*, meaning simply 'child', and that would be used until she displayed some trait or physical characteristic which identified her, or if her play with sounds became more purposeful and one or two syllables particularly amused her. "Doo-chaa" had made her chuckle, and was the word for 'little', so Ducha she became.

Ducha's spoken language would grow from all the inner needs of a dependent infant, just as the communication of her hominin and early human ancestors had done. Within her second year, however, Ducha's appetite for words suddenly became insatiable;[4] the compulsion to develop verbal skills *fast* seemed extraordinary.

~~~~~~~~~

Why?

The cause could have lain with the glacial periods which had occurred long before. During the preceding 400,000 years[5] the climate swirled from one 100-thousand-year cycle of cold to the next, with sudden, brief 10,000-thousand year episodes of warmer temperatures in between. It was against this turbulent backdrop that our own species began to emerge. So whatever lifestyle adaptations the earliest *Homo sapiens* had been managing to come up with, that was what confronted their new-born infants. Yet again they were the species' most vulnerable individuals, the ones who would have to survive childhood if they were to breed; yet again they were under pressure.

As so many times before, the great ice ages made the African landscape cool and dry. Plants were the first of the foodstuffs to be affected, along with the insects and animals that lived off their flowers, fruit, leaves, bark or roots. Early *Homo sapiens* people had moved in response, going to lower altitudes, sheltered valleys and anywhere they could still forage according to familiar patterns. When the temperature dropped too low or too quickly, however, these kinds of food sources simply disappeared. Fewer and fewer plants were available, either for the people themselves, or for the creatures that came and in their turn, provided nourishment. Eventually it was only the toughest of the grasses and small scrubby bushes that were able to withstand the relentless aridity and the
~~~~~~~~~

areas where they grew expanded, taking over from the woodlands.

Some wildlife could cope, though. Herds of grazing animals capable of digesting and thriving on the wide barren landscape began to multiply, and the people turned their attention to these, improving their ability to scavenge and hunt on the cool savannahs. At least, the adults did. In the past, once infants were reasonably mobile they could trail alongside their elders and begin to forage and gather food for themselves; they had to learn what to look for and where, but largely they didn't need adults to do it for them.

All that changed during the ice ages. When, in the past, meat had been an occasional bounty, infants would certainly have had to sidle in and get a share, but once meat took over as the main source of food, infants could only stand by and watch. They could neither obtain the meat nor light the fires which tenderized it for them to eat. What confronted them then was total dependency. Not only did they go on needing physical protection while small and at risk, under these circumstances they also needed to be fed long past weaning. Infants would only survive if others were willing to prepare and share meat with them – not just for months, but for years. When tired hunters returned hungry from the chase, the young could be very low down indeed in the pecking order.

In a hard world natural selection had always made short work of eliminating from a clan's gene pool those who, in childhood, weren't able to find ways of getting themselves looked after. Now the issue was even more basic – getting themselves fed, and ensuring that they went on getting fed. The strategy had to begin early, and it had to be sustainable.

What that strategy was could have started like this: as soon as infants vocalised in response to the people around, babble might adopt a lower pitch if fathers were nearby, higher for mothers. Such an instinctive reaction was perhaps the human equivalent of the submissive postures adopted by the young of many animal species, as they sensed the hierarchies of the pack. In the young of these early modern ancestors, of course, changing posture wasn't an option – physically, they just couldn't oblige. The voice would have to do the work. And it would have to do more. Adult communication was now very different from the simple emotive expressions of earlier species; in a baby's earliest months emotive expressions would do very well, but his needs would change – and he'd soon become aware that what he was hearing around him were sound patterns being used purposefully, specifically, and they were carried on a tune.

Suddenly the whole idea 'clicked'. He would try to sound like those around, using their tunes. And word-like units could flow in these intonation patterns – forming a kind of 'jargon'. Then, almost overnight he would recognize the special power of real words and begin to learn as many as possible as quickly as possible, and try using them for himself.

This is easily seen in today's children - the stage (usually at around 16 to 24 months) is marked by the dramatic appearance of a host of useful words: "more!" "sausage!" "juice!"…and an insatiable appetite for adding new ones

In our ancestors, infants were totally dependent on being accepted and nurtured by the group – so they managed, albeit subconsciously, by trying to sound like them.[6] Put simply, the faster they learned to talk, the better chances they had of getting fed.

The brain – young and flexible as it was – met the challenge: a diet high in animal protein did have its good points – and of course, at some stage, there would have been FOXP2. If its attributes could be brought to bear on communication, then infants would have been the first to press it into service. Understanding quickly what others said, and amassing vocabulary day by day – that was the key to success.

~~~~~~~~

Fortunately for Ducha's people, food was once again plentiful, varied and at least some of it was easily obtained by older children. But for infants, their race towards socially competent communication was still being run at break-neck speed; the original pressure had been remorseless, and its urgency would be indelible.

Not that Ducha's thirst for understanding and her drive to express herself were tense affairs – far from it. Her abilities grew day by day, through the casual interplay with those around, and it would be those vital aspects of spoken language which naturally permeated human relationships that would so often be well to the fore, and which she was already primed to absorb.

Exploring the situation in the living areas under the gum trees, Ducha was now walking. Somewhat unsteadily, she would take herself off to this or that
~~~~~~~~

familiar figure when they were nearby, or head towards them when they came back into the clearing. Her smile and happy efforts to talk went down well and it was a good start.

Early modern society would have been a test for any small child though, not least because of its genetic diversity. Inevitably, this showed itself in ways apart from talents which had beneficial, practical applications; it also highlighted individual personality.[7] Each family member came across differently, and might react differently towards Ducha according to circumstance. She put out feelers. To be nurtured, protected and fed for the long period when she would be reliant on others, Ducha had to try and fit in with them all, and that would mean gauging not just status, but temperament, mood and attitude, and to present herself pleasingly.

Indeed, so powerful was the motivation to do this, that at two years old she could adapt the way she communicated according to who her listener was,[8] so finding her place in a close, inner circle of family wasn't too hard. Day by day of course her horizons were widening, and below her consciousness this necessary and subtle fact gathering about people was extending its reach.

Fortunately, the company of the other children in Kipanga's big family was already providing Ducha with the ideal preparation for its diverse characters and changeable relationships. As she gained confidence, play became the natural way to investigate this human jungle, but it didn't obey set times, impose age restrictions or confine itself to one place – it just happened. So little ones might scramble over and around family members of all ages as they awoke, rested or carried out tasks,[9] and if inclined, anyone could enjoy this relaxing process. Taking her cues from older children helped Ducha find out how far she could go with this or that individual.

For their own part, and getting to know her, they'd soothed her inevitable tantrums when weaning started, coaxed her back when she'd strayed too far from the family group, and now as she negotiated her third year they were her playmates in the more energetic games typical of young primates – and humans. To start with she merely watched, almost hanging back and retreating to the women and babies if she felt intimidated. But gradually she sensed when she could join in, and her understanding of the dynamics of social encounters took more steps forward. The games were tactile, physical, interactive and enjoyable, and nothing demonstrated contrasts in personality quite so explicitly. Many involved turn-taking, imitation and repetition (the processes which would incidentally foster her spoken language too), so she had ample opportunity for seeing who it was that kept activities going or wound them down: who approved or protested, who made mischief or cheated and who played fair, who was rejected and who was liked.

Behaviour wasn't the only source of information, though. Ducha's perception of this or that playmate's moods, attitudes or preferences drew on many sources: body posture, the expression of eyes, the creasing of forehead, the droop or curl of lips, slight tightening or relaxation around the mouth – the face threw light on its owner's mind and feelings, and, of course, the meanings of what they said.

And it was Ducha's satisfied, sad or happy demeanour which told Hiba whether her young daughter was getting on in this boisterous company. Mostly she was, and when energy levels flagged and the little girl rested beside Hiba, her mother would talk with her about what had gone on.

As she grew up, though, comments gradually began to focus on her companions rather than the games. It was they who were the source of interest.

"Chiku not play," she said one day, "she cry, she cry."

Hiba said, "Was she hurt…?"

Ducha shook her head, frowning.

"She cry, she crying, not stop. Mama Chiku come."

Hiba nodded. Everyone was conscious that Chiku was making a lot of fuss these days. Her mother had recently given birth and the older child was jealous. It was a small but significant step forward that Ducha had been perplexed by Chiku's mysterious tears, but like so much that occurred in relation to human communication, its arrival was registered quietly, in the deep dark networks of the brain.

More than that, however, Ducha was reaching beyond the natural self-centredness of infancy, dimly detecting that others too had feelings, that they might have different needs from her own. It was the first whisper of empathy, a move towards seeing another's point of view.[10] Such understanding was slow-growing, but when Ducha turned to someone for help or company, picking up on their emotional state would make her better prepared for their reaction. And this ability to pick up on another's perspective was worth hanging on to: in a mixed community depending mostly on concerted action in order to survive, how tortuously would consensus be achieved if such a capacity were lacking?

~~~~~~~~
~~~~~~~~

Perhaps it was one further critical aspect of communication which was strengthened during this time. For early modern people, like their predecessors, it was vital to interpret the behaviour patterns of both predator and prey, and by extension, intuitively, they'd do the same with each other – the mirror neurons in the brain would see to that. Taking account of mood or disposition enabled them to respond in ways that served their own best interests. Posture, gesture, facial expression – and tone of voice – would all make their point.

More was probably being demanded of the system now, though. If people were dissimilar, with their own agendas, allowances had to be made. Spoken language had to reach down into a deeper level of understanding to make a connection with the minds of others. The first place it encountered this challenge was obviously childhood, and if a suitably flexible approach wasn't established then, juvenile and adult communication could grind to a halt. It wasn't enough to express a comment, a reaction, an instruction, however adequately; the successful speaker engaged with his listeners, and did so in the light of how they might feel.

But there was a darker side. Deceptive behavioural ploys were practiced by other primates, and falsehood could and would insinuate itself into human communication. Spoken language, in its egalitarian way, had to make room for the bad as well as the good.

~~~~~~~~

Yet as Ducha was also to discover, some situations showed themselves stubbornly resistant to the charms of spoken language. Every now and then
~~~~~~~~

one of the children would, for reasons perhaps unknown even to himself, react obstructively – kick or barge without provocation – disrupt the flow of the running or climbing or rough and tumble which normally kept them amused. Strong personalities could clash. Then there seemed no adequate verbal response, no spoken communication to cover such extremes. When tempers flared the fights began silently, erupting into screams and shouts that brought care-givers running as violence set in.

Adults sorted these squabbles, physically separating the children, keeping them apart until calm returned, although finding a better solution to such disturbances would be elusive when anger really couldn't be contained. Sometimes what was said was more animal than verbal, even if it did have a word-like shape. If emotion was raw, spoken language was out of its depth.

For the most part, though, from infancy to maturity, Ducha's spoken language *could* fulfil a very important role. Where feelings and emotions were the low-key stuff of every-day occurrences, sensitive communication allowed these to be shared, and this added dimension had meant sensing that it wasn't just what was said that mattered, but how she said it. It also meant she would listen, giving attention in return, hearing the person behind what was being said.

Spoken language would be central to Ducha's life with her kinsfolk.

~~~~~~~~

Imperceptibly, a process was at work which overcame the solitariness of the individual, bonding
~~~~~~~~

him into his group, an affirmation reassuringly like the close tender stroking of long ago. Talking for its own sake – taking pleasure in the sense of communion which it fostered – that nurtured everyone, old and young alike.[11]

Perhaps there were other pleasures too.

Around the caves and shelters near the coast and in the warm hinterland, the family groups which made up these early modern clans were building a collective way of living. When it was good and they rested content, perhaps other aspects of their existence found their way from mind to lips, as something shared, like delicacies at a feast.

Life was shot through with emotion, and human encounters didn't hold a monopoly on the arousal of pleasure, fear or anger – after all, responding to the natural environment had always been as close as breathing. So did they use their speech to share a welling-up of wonder in the world around them? The moonlight shining on the sea? The sudden iridescence of a sunbird's wings? The greening of the landscape after rain…

Such reactions, rising as instant evaluations of what they perceived, might generate enjoyment – one aspect of many sensations which would register on a pain-to-pleasure scale. A sense of beauty with words to express it would emerge one day, but when?

Maybe 90,000 years ago attending to life's necessities was still too demanding. An everyday vocabulary revolving solely around the social and practical functions might have been all that was needed. But spoken language wouldn't stagnate – lifestyles continued to change, and with that came the possibility of further growth.

If there was discontent or restlessness, or a population outgrowing its habitat, then groups of the people would have to move away. It happened about 10,000 years later, when the sea once more shrank down with the cold. Then the narrow straits at the mouth of the Red Sea allowed people to leave Africa altogether,[12] just as the Erectus before them had done. Some didn't go though, and for a very lucky few of their descendants, the place to be was somewhere near its heart, in the Great Rift Valley again; what these people were faced with may well have been significant, and may well have needed spoken language to grow again.

<u>The seedbed for spoken language…</u>
- Infants had to integrate quickly into their close extended families, picking up on a range of cues including oral communication.
- This now used a wide repertoire of speech sounds, and perceiving and attaching meaning to these was underpinned by the early sapiens on-going necessity of interpreting a host of environmental sounds.
- Profound and lengthened dependency on adults continued to drive infants to become competent communicators as fast as possible.
- Exploiting an ability to empathise influenced the way spoken language was expressed, enabling individuals to become effective and acceptable communicators within their group. In adulthood this skill would be necessary when lifestyles demanded cooperation both within and between human groups.

CHAPTER 14

Feeling the Pressure

Physically Modern People…74,000 years ago

It was happening again, but this time the cloud that stole across the landscape created a darkness that lasted for months.

A clan of four families, each of about 30 individuals, had been occupying a region of savannah about 100k east of the longest lake in the western arm of the Rift Valley, and to begin with had expected the gloom to lift following storms. But it hadn't. The sun never broke through, and as the days wore on into weeks then months, the air cooled, plant food began to fail and the animals who browsed and grazed on it wandered away from their habitual places.

It hadn't taken long for the clan likewise to desert its cluster of seasonal bases – small stands of trees surrounded by loose circles of spiky acacia branches, cut down and laid there as protection. They headed in the direction of wooded slopes to the north-west, but even here the lack of sunlight unbalanced the normal predictable rhythms of flora and fauna. Before long the families were on the move again, retreating further into the hills.

Among them there was no-one who could remember anything like this happening before; so they moved out of instinct, partly triggered by the dwindling food sources and partly a residual feeling that the forest was where safety lay. So they stayed for as long as there were grubs, insects, reptiles and small mammals to be had, and then they pushed on.

For tiny infants the disruption was minimal, but for children old enough to have ideas about what to expect each day, the shifting disturbed them; between their second and third years they were really getting to grips with what went on and didn't like the changes – or the atmosphere of fear afflicting their families.

Kitunda was trudging fretfully behind his elder brother during what was the third relocation in as many weeks. He was robust and energetic, but for a child just short of four years old the trek deep into mountainous forest was exhausting. When they stopped to rest Kitunda pulled on his brother's arm.

"What look for? What do in trees?"

He'd asked the same question umpteen times.

"Find food," answered the boy irritably.

Kitunda opened his mouth to ask again, because the answer didn't make sense. They'd always had food at the edge of the savannah without all of them having to climb steep slopes and push their way through bushes and plants, vines and trees. His brother saw the question coming.

"Go ask Mama."

But Kitunda's mother was distressed herself, scared by the unyielding sombre skies.

"Look for food," she said helplessly.

Kitunda knew there was more to it. He felt rather like he did when watching his brother prise a grub from its hole using just the right kind of twig – one with a thorn to impale the creature. He couldn't do it and it was the same frustration.

"What we do *here,* not on big land?"

His mother shrugged.

"Food gone, not there now," she said.

There was a finality about her answer which only upset Kitunda more. The aggravation of not understanding was coupled with fear over his mother's apparent inability to help him. Angry sobs tangled with more efforts at finding the right kind of question to prise out an answer that satisfied him. He tried a different tack.

"Kitunda *tired...* Food *here*? Stop here now....? Kitunda *tired....*"

This time she stopped and sat down with him on her lap, burying his head in her arms, and although the sobs ceased then, Kitunda's insecurity remained.

When eventually the group's route took them downhill and they could see a glimmer of water, they realised this was as far as they could go. A lake spread before them, vast and turbulent as the sea. Its western limits were beyond the horizon, and on either side its shores stretched away into the spray-filled distance. It was their good fortune that here in the lee of the mountain range they'd crossed, the rainforest was thick enough to shield them from the worst effects of the cloud, spawned by a catastrophic volcanic eruption far away across the Indian Ocean.

~~~~~~~~

There, on the island of Sumatra, Mt Toba had split the heavens apart,[1] and at a stroke its consequences would decimate the descendants of those migrant people who had left Africa perhaps 6000 years before. There was the blanket of suffocating ash that covered every living thing for hundreds of kilometres, and the high sulphurous haze reflecting the heat of the sun away from the earth, so that the cold would eliminate completely those who had reached the more northerly
~~~~~~~~

latitudes. Even the tough Neanderthals, a species of human supremely adapted to cold climates, and whose lineage had diverged 200,000 or more years before – even these might have had to call it a day; by 71,000 years ago they had retreated south to the edge of the eastern Mediterranean.[2] On the continent of Africa itself, it would only be those people in its tropical interior, those who had found refuge in sheltered, protective havens, who could hide until it was safe to come out.

~~~~~~~

On the first evening, after the group had fed on what instinct gauged to be edible, they gathered at the edge of the forest, the first time for many weeks they'd had an open vista before them. The cloud cover seemed thinner than before, but in the halo surrounding the faint disc of the sun, as they watched its slow slide, strange colours reflected off the waters of the lake. Browns and livid yellows made the sky sickly, and did nothing to reassure either them or Kitunda.

Everything about the place was utterly unfamiliar, and he tried again to bring some order to his confusion. But his 'what' questions and his 'where' questions left him as disheartened as ever, and now a less familiar, vague interrogative burst out as he teetered on the brink of tears once more:

'Waa...ee....?'

The wailing of a child in the dusk had to be stopped. In the forest – and particularly at its edge – nocturnal hunters might approach unseen; on the savannah the people had had some warning. Here everyone was uneasy.
~~~~~~~

Kitunda's mother shushed him till he was calmer, then, responding to the rising and falling of his appeal to her, began.

"Big cloud come.... Lots of days, sun hide.... Leaves fall, bushes no leaves, animals gone."

Kitunda gazed at his mother with fixed concentration. She went on,

"We go in woods, find fruit.... Sun still hide.... No more fruit, no berries.... Trees all dry"

She rubbed her fingers together and Kitunda nodded. By contrast it was still humid in the rainforest, despite the cooling of the air, and here the canopy allowed moisture to remain at the lower levels in the ferns and mosses.

"But here big forest ... Food here, stay here now."

Kitunda nodded again. He had understood while his mother talked, and sat for a few moments trying to pull it all together in one place inside his head. But his memory for so long a narrative hadn't been able to keep up. He would have to get his mother to repeat it. What had worked, like a twig with a thorn, was saying "why".

Not crying now, though still feeling anxious, Kitunda copied what he'd said,

"Why...? Why...we...here now....?"

And patiently his mother went over what had led to Kitunda's family suddenly altering the patterns of many lifetimes. For her too the interaction had been demanding. She'd drawn on an ability to recall past events, and had had to hunt for images in her mind. She sorted them, then described them to Kitunda in order, and the technique seemed to do the trick. To her relief she saw his sense of security gradually restored.

The question and its reply were repeated on subsequent days – exactly the same narrative, because Kitunda's mother could only do it this way. In any case, it fitted in with the liking for repetition which came so naturally to children, and which care-givers were used to providing. Soon the explanation stuck, and Kitunda gained in confidence. He also found he'd hit on an additional way of furnishing himself with knowledge about everything.[3] Asking 'why' was less specific than 'who' or 'where' or 'what', but care-givers usually answered because of the context and his querying voice. He resembled the pups of wild dogs, nuzzling at adults to regurgitate food, craving nourishment, only this was of the intellectual kind.

~~~~~~~~

Parents today will often relate tales of their children's questions. It's a phase of infancy that expands along with their curiosity, and many a care-giver will admit to feelings of baffled inadequacy at the topics they can suddenly be presented with.

"Daddy, how big is the wind?"

"Why doesn't the earth fall out of the sky..?"

Adult spoken language is prodded (and prodded again) to come up with a suitable answer – and it is infants, not adults, who are the motivators. Just as in earlier times, the young will flourish best if there's a responsive interplay between themselves and those caring for them.

~~~~~~~~

In this new place Kitunda's questions probed what his family was having to do to survive in unforeseen conditions – ones that taxed every ounce of their ingenuity.

Previously, the routines of living had barely needed more than casual self-direction, and it was only higher profile expeditions that involved plans being repeatedly outlined beforehand – but not in response to 'why'. Cognitive abilities had to have stretched and forged links in thinking before 'why' could work. Now, though, maybe its time had come.

Here the group was extremely wary, confined as it was between lake and rainforest. As week followed week and the temperature became cooler, the challenges bore down on Kitunda's elders and slowly new patterns of activity replaced those which had been habitual down on the savannah.

Around the places in the forest where they had gone searching for food, their feet had trampled the vegetation into pathways, and their talk flitted across the glades they'd cleared. In itself the sound of their own voices was a comfort, and often what they talked about mattered little, because vagueness had its value too. They still sang when darkness fell, and when they beat the trees or the ground it was like an act of defiance in the face of the eerie sallow moon. Then their voices began blending together, rising louder and louder, and the people ceased to be a cluster of frightened, anxious individuals. The singing and dancing made each of them feel part of something much bigger, part of a much stronger whole.

Come daylight, ideas about where and how they might forage for food found their way into speech.[4] Possibilities could be talked through before any of the group risked life or limb; when they combined their intellectual resources in this way they were likely to be more effective than if they had acted alone. They were by necessity getting more out of the spoken language currently available, and the practice strengthened the skill; when a foray or search was over, its details formed a sequence to be retold, and now narratives flowed with greater ease.

In spite of their best efforts however, amidst the looming trees and the dense undergrowth the family's diet was restricted; they were missing out on the grassland plants and animal protein. They simply couldn't use the hunting and scavenging techniques which worked so well on the savannah. To add to their discomfort, the resources available were expertly plundered by other primates – the gorillas, chimpanzees, monkeys and smallish baboons who outnumbered Kitunda's family and its clan in the ridges and valleys behind the lake. As the forests dwindled all were forced to compete. But the people rediscovered what could be rustled out from under the dark canopy, and now they had weapons. Sometimes when replacements weren't forthcoming, they made use of the tough reeds growing in profusion near the water's edge. These could be fashioned and made sharp as any stone, so after a while some meat did reappear, in the shape of giant rats and other rodents, and of course, the occasional competitor.

Talking about what to do and how to do it accelerated the rate at which the people adapted to their privations. And imperceptibly, during the protracted winter they endured, the shape and fluency of spoken language complied with the demands made upon it.

Kitunda and his young kin, hearing utterances that stretched their powers of recall, and spoken language covering more aspects of living than ever before, had no idea that this was new. They just did their best to keep pace, and in the course of experimentation, began to add some refinements of their own.[5]

Communication between older members of the family was competent and adequate, meeting their needs. But did it meet the needs of the young, hungry for experience 'by proxy'? Several of them had been about the same age, between two and four years old when the volcanic winter struck, and although hardly a desirable event, was just the sort of stimulus to their understanding and self-expression likely to spark and establish further developments. It was good timing.

~~~~~~~~

It was also fortunate that FOXP2 had come when it did. Spoken language had increasingly capitalised on the fact that articulatory agility could provide subtle alterations that signalled subtle shades of meanings – and this was turning out to be a veritable wellspring.

For example, "Kitunda get nice leaves" could mean something he'd done, or happened to be doing, or even was about to do. But pull the sounds around a bit, insert a few extra syllables - "Kitunda's got..." or "Kitunda's getting..." or "Kitunda'll get... nice leaves" and his words would come out more precisely in line with what he wanted to convey. In itself such a speech habit might seem trifling, but with its passion for organisation, the brain was sketching out another faint blue-print, a pliant supporting framework for surer ways to indicate past occurrence, an ongoing situation, or a future intention. It might well be grabbed by those growing
~~~~~~~~

up in uncertain circumstances if it had the effect of increasing a sense of security. Spoken language had a feed-back function – what you heard yourself say was as important as what others said. But trifling though the subtle alterations to words or phrases might appear, the feature added another layer of complexity – something probably best tackled by a young brain with plenty of adaptability at its disposal.

~~~~~~~

As it transpired, there would have been plenty of time for the innovation to get off the ground. Not until Kitunda was nine years old did signs begin to suggest that the worst was over. Then his family crept tentatively out onto the savannah again. It was still cold, and the vicious dry atmosphere carried on nibbling at the woods and forests, enlarging the savannah areas as it had always done. The herds of antelope and zebra, the lions, leopards and cheetahs, the buffalo and the elephants, they and countless other species had diminished – the rolling grasslands were parched and empty of the teeming wildlife so familiar to Kitunda's family. The numbers would slowly build up once more, but it would be another thousand years before warmer temperatures returned.

Like the animals, the human population had become sparse and scattered, and as Kitunda's family groups tried to resume their way of life it was soon clear that other clans had disappeared and an immense loneliness descended on them, dogging them like the shadow of the looming cloud. When they moved from place to place it was always as much in the hope of sighting other humans as in
~~~~~~~

tracking down food. Scouting parties were greeted with intense interest on their return, and stories of what they had seen and done partly kept the sense of isolation at bay, whiling away their times of rest.

But the stories got more interesting. As Kitunda and the younger individuals matured and accompanied the forays, how they gave their own accounts owed much to their early enhanced focus on talking, and the way it had led to a richer style of relating experiences; in the hands of a generation less burdened by the practical aspects of the family's altered circumstances, spoken language could capture attention, entertain and raise everyone's spirits.

~~~~~~~~

Apart from the infiltration into speech of ways to map actions into a time-frame, the telling and retelling of exploits had been obliged to nudge spoken language into tidying up its act. Phrase had followed phrase in traditional fashion, with neutral utterances linking them loosely, borne along on underlying rhythms and tunes. What had happened of late was that even these small features could impress some additional shade of meaning onto the words they accompanied.[6] 'And' was the most straightforward –

"We saw elephants 'nd warthog" – it had been useful just in making a list. It could also join a sequence of actions smoothly: "We tracked warthog 'nd we killed one." Then there was 'then', which neatly clarified further the order in which things happened "…then we scared off vultures…"

In a rush of excitement, speech was shaping expressions like 'because' and 'so that' in order to
~~~~~~~~

explain a proposition; it provided the 'ifs and buts' to convey doubt; it inserted 'or' to lay out a choice. They were little things, syllables and combinations of syllables which took a fraction of a second to slip in, but their contribution elucidated and added momentum – that extra energy allowing spoken language to go faster and further if it so desired.[7] And it had so desired. The Kitunda generation had been young children in a highly charged atmosphere; when they most needed to comprehend and communicate, that was when their neural circuitry had been ready and willing to come to their aid.

In the great span of human history, it hadn't always been like that. There had been long periods when the form of spoken language would be settled, perfectly suited to the needs of its users; then something would crop up obliging it to change. It was like a living thing – like a plant needing particular amounts of sunlight, moisture and nutrients in order to bloom and bear fruit. The evolution of spoken language had gone through times when it might have seemed dormant, but then there would be sudden spurts of growth, then nothing except perhaps roots spreading out unseen. Eventually a moment of blooming might arrive with its promise of fruit and proliferation. For the generation of people living in the aftermath of the Mt. Toba eruption this could have been one such moment.

Spoken language had come a long way with its simple grammatical structures – its short, variable phrases which could link up. It was well-supported by intonation, facial expression and other non-verbal devices. In the main, the way a speaker modulated his voice suggested the kind of response required, and emphasis signalled what was important. It had been a style well suited to conveying the basics – the dynamics affecting relationships that Ducha had had to pick up on – and fine for the practicalities of daily living, something short, unequivocal, relating to the here and now.

But agile articulation could insert meanings all over the place, and young speakers were no more aware of the "rules" of language than the rules of anything else – in play children experimented, threw, slid, climbed and broke things that adults used quite differently. So the young tried out whatever intricacies of language occurred to them, and pushed grammar into improvising.[8]

The sudden life-style changes forced on people by the events of 74,000 years ago inevitably upset their infants, and in their verbal interplay, caregivers would respond as best they could, each prompting more from the other: it was the same mutual stimulus for new vocal behaviour as had set the process off in the first place. So for young and old alike, the system was extending itself. By adulthood spoken language might become more syntactic, capable of conveying meaningful detail through arrangements of sounds, words and phrases - and probably sentences.[9]

Back out in the cool dry savannah, the spoken language of these physically modern people would be different from before - a human adaptation to adverse circumstances. So as the years passed, the ultimate fate of this growth surge – if indeed that's what occurred - would rest on whether 'favourable' conditions were forthcoming - whether infants would continue to need their vocal powers to secure attention, gather information, and seek an understanding of *why* things happened. Would there have been the motivation if Kitunda and his family had been able to return to their former routine lifestyle? It's hard to say.

Yet when change occurred within so short a time-span, less than a human lifetime, talking about it, about what they did or might do – just *talking* - was almost the only positive approach available. And there's a tantalising possibility that the kind of event which these people experienced might have had a permanent effect on the genetic legacy they left.

The field of epigenetics looks at how external factors can cause genes to alter how they function – what they influence, even though the genes themselves stay the same,[10] and research has suggested a curious possibility. Children may be affected by an environmental incident occurring during a critical period of their grandparents' lives – something which 'switched' particular genes on or off.[11] If this is the case, then maybe spoken language was the beneficiary of such a biological feature. Talking really could have helped during the crisis, and any genetic input thus activated might have remained in place, ready to be passed on.

~~~~~~~~

In global terms the African population probably fared better than elsewhere after the eruption, but there is a marked scarcity of archaeological evidence for where they were and what they did up until nearly 50,000 years ago. This is a witness to how fragile their hold on existence really was. After this time, though, evidence for new kinds of behaviour can be found – cultural activities – and
~~~~~~~~

there is agreement that the presence of spoken language can be implied. Perhaps the fact that these people survived at all is thanks to spoken language.

<u>The seedbed for spoken language...</u>
- Children old enough to demand explanations for situations they didn't understand challenged care-givers to find ways to meet that need. The interplay between them fostered the growth of longer, more complex narratives.
- Limitations in attention-span continued to influence the ability of spoken language to still be concise and yet carry more detail, and grammatical features would emerge to fulfil that role.
- Children's pleasure in repetition helped to establish robust auditory memory – a necessary requirement as story-telling offered a way of dealing with life's events.
- Their own longer narratives would gradually become fluent.
- Their experience of the reassurance and value of spoken language may have included a genetic element, further strengthening its contribution to the survival of the human species.

CHAPTER 15

Equipped for a Future

Homo sapiens - Fully Modern People... 45,000 years ago.

Whatever the strategies for survival had been during those hard times, eventually populations recovered, and the people who emerged displayed characteristics that can now be defined as fully modern – people like us.

Several times temperatures had climbed and fallen during the years leading up to 50,000 years ago and season by season the people's resilience and stamina had gone on being tested. Now, though, by about 45,000 years ago, the climate had stabilised somewhat. It was cool and dry, and in an ironic twist, the Great Rift Valley in East Africa, littered with the mountainous evidence of its own successive volcanic eruptions, renewed its offer of resources in its strings of lakes, its woodlands, savannahs and fickle rivers. Among other locations in the world, it was here that evidence of a human presence appears again.

This was a landscape where, ever since they stood on two feet and walked, people had been shaped.

Now they were tall – men reaching about 1.75m in height, women perhaps 14cms shorter. Their build was relatively slim, a reminder of concessions made in the past during hot climatic cycles, and tucked below a high vertical forehead their face was quite short, with a small nose and distinct chin.[1] Inside the skull the brain had concerned itself with orchestrating the humming networks, and either because slow, incremental cognitive advances had brought them to a new threshold, or due to the timely input from a genetic mutation again, these people began behaving differently from their predecessors. There are varying views on how long ago any genetic basis for modern human behaviours originated – including spoken language – with a range of between 190,000 and 50,000 years highlighting the uncertainty.

What is clear though, is that in the past, physiological and behavioural adaptations had each regulated the other – what they did affected their bodies, then their bodies could alter what they did, and so on. Yet after 50,000 years ago, although physically they stayed much the same, their capabilities really took off.[2] It was a dramatic contrast in the pattern of human evolution.

Inevitably, when they awoke in the morning, eating and avoiding being eaten was still a constant concern. Equally, negotiating, building and maintaining relationships would be the dynamic which underpinned a clan's success. However, if the ancestral communication system had been weaving itself through early human lifestyles, particularly during the tough isolation of earlier years,[3] the possible influence of that can hardly be ignored. It could even have been the effects of spoken language, working like a catalyst, that were now galvanising the rate at which radical new attributes were emerging. Among these, the archaeological record shows the earliest appearance of what can be described as art; there's rapid change in the diversity of artefacts – and in the materials used; and there are signs suggesting the appearance of ceremony, and burial of the dead.

Motivated to express themselves from the moment they were born, people had grown up sharing feelings, information, misinformation and plans, and in answer to such clamour spoken language had carried on propagating its own internal and self-supporting framework. Talking had helped them cope even when they'd been deprived of the wider social interactions when populations were more dense, but as opportunities slowly increased for rebuilding these fractured links, spoken language would be impatient to get going again – it had a hunger of its own.

It was almost just because the very act of speaking gave pleasure.[4] Like the enjoyment of food there was more than one dimension to it. It had practical applications, certainly, but there was also a sensual satisfaction in the way sounds tripped off the tongue. It was felt and heard at one and the same time, and a novel expression could delight both speaker and listeners in the interplay of sound and meaning. Talking mattered.

There was also another curious distinction which language enjoyed, and maybe this too played a part in the cognitive and cultural leaps forward that mark this period in our history. Typically, the momentum for development is at its most powerful in the young – indeed it has been the basis for this perspective on language evolution. But to gain the prominence it has achieved in humans, spoken language has gone one better. It continues to expand and develop beyond childhood.

~~~~~~~~

Coming down from the hills in search of food, the Makwetu clans-women would, from time to time,
~~~~~~~~

encounter foragers from a nearby woodland group. Today they'd both converged on an area of mainly deciduous trees, and several patches of fungi had been found. To the Makwetu women the fungi were unfamiliar, and they were instantly inquisitive to find out if they were edible. So they watched the others while the plump delicacies were picked, listening attentively to the name. Then echoed what they heard. It was also going to be necessary to know how to prepare them – whether the fungi needed cooking – and with a mixture of questioning words, gestures and miming the problem was soon solved.

Engaged in searching and collecting alongside each other, and with their children in tow, a bond grew quite quickly among the women. There was a reassuring similarity in how infants and young children sought attention and in the vocal reactions of their care-givers, and this spread a degree of understanding which compensated for their limited conversation, especially when there was cause for laughter. Older children soon found games to play, and when the groups parted to go their separate ways, progress seemed to have been made, the Makwetu women taking with them both a new word and the start of friendships.

~~~~~~~~

Totally new words – completely original combinations of sounds – were probably quite rare additions to the adult vocabulary.[5] Each clan had its own perfectly serviceable expressions for features of its environment, but if something turned up that one group didn't know, someone else's word would do very nicely – as in the case of the fungi. Even if old individuals reminisced that once upon a time
~~~~~~~~

they'd eaten just such a thing, their word for it would almost certainly give way to the recent one.

What also flowed particularly freely, when parties of men or women from the clans met up, weren't actually expressions relating to the material world outside, but their casual greetings and how they dealt with what went on within themselves. As they relaxed and observed spoken language applying to personal and social situations, sometimes one clan's expressions seem to fit more closely the intentions of the speaker, and these would creep into the listeners' everyday usage, displacing the original.[6]

Words and phrases constantly risked being inexact reflections of what was a highly individual perception of life – and the recipient of a thought thus conveyed stood a fair chance of getting it wrong. Yet the interdependence of people was crucial to staying alive, and required effective tools to help them rub along. It was therefore the vocabulary of attitudes, ideas, opinions and feelings, and turns of phrase for reasoning, persuading and exercising the will that accumulated most readily.[7]

~~~~~~~~~

As the months passed, with the benefits of familiarity and friendship, both the woodland clan and Makwetu's clan saw their numbers increase, and if their association continued to be close enough for them to merge, so, eventually would their ways of speaking.[8] At the start, though, in each clan there would be individuals who would now learn to be fluent in a language that had originated elsewhere and so differed from their own – for the
~~~~~~~~~

same reasons that had motivated Hiba to hone her communication skills thousands of years before. It would be more difficult now because language itself had become complex, and despite all their best efforts, incomers could always be identified by their accent. The tunes that characterised a particular language were absorbed so early in life that no later technique could prime the ear to listen in the way that came with ease to the clans' new-born babies.

Makwetu's grandson Kigoma, now six months old, was already registering the characteristic patterns of the way the old man talked. The clans had relocated to an area further north where caves offered shelter during the wetter season, and Makwetu was sitting under an overhang, chatting to his daughter. The baby finished feeding, and because he was heavy, Zina laid him down on a soft hide while she gazed out over the flat land between the cliffs and a lake. Satisfied and aware of the voices, Kigoma gurgled and babbled, playing with the sounds and sensations.

Not surprisingly, the legacy of sounds at his disposal was also a good deal richer than that of his ancient predecessors.[9] The ebb and flow of populations, with their diverse repertoires of speech sounds, had left their marks by way of temporary tracks in every infant descendant's brain. So the vast fund of tongue and lip placement, direction and expulsion of air was available to Kigoma, and all he had to do was have a good go at them over the next few months, find out which ones matched what he was hearing, repeat them into permanency, then forget about the rest.[10] Considering that his own versions lacked the sonority of those made by people with low larynxes, it was up to his brain to recognise when his related to theirs, which of course it did. Remarkably, even at this age, the finer points of familiar vowels were winning over unfamiliar ones, and by the time Kigoma was a year old, consonants bereft of meaning (the ones nobody used) had disappeared altogether.

Zina picked him up again, patting his back and enjoying the feel of his warm skin. She'd heard the babbling and answered – taking turns with him as if it were a conversation. Suddenly her attention was distracted by the appearance of a herd of reedbuck. They were moving slowly, grazing on the damp grass at the edge of the trees. Both she and Makwetu stiffened, staying still and silent and she shifted the baby so that he was more likely to fall asleep.

Another good reason for Makwetu's choice of location – this was an ideal vantage point from which to prey on certain of the herd animals. In the other caves, back from the long ledge, several men were collecting their weapons then padding softly along to where a path would take them round and out of sight of the reedbuck, into the woodland where they would have cover for stalking.

From where Makwetu sat he could view it all, and he had already been joined by a nephew of about thirteen years old, Rubama, who crept to his side as soon as he detected the soft flurry of activity round the caves. Makwetu glanced down at him, acknowledging his presence and the reason for it. The youth was there to pick his brains.

"They're nervous," he whispered, nodding towards the animals. "See their tails..?"

Rubama marked the detail, concentrating, saying nothing till the twitching ceased, then he breathed "Settled now…?" looking at Makwetu for confirmation.

The old man nodded, and the pair continued throughout the lengthy process of gauging moments, assessing distance, evaluating risk. At every step (and during the interminable pauses when, to the boy's intense frustration, nothing happened at all), Makwetu's whispers sought to reign in his natural impatience and explain why it all demanded so much care. From early on Rubama had been sensitive to how animals behaved – obeying the age-old instinct to second-guess the intentions of predators – but the balance of power had shifted and *being* the predator demanded an alteration in perspectives. Makwetu knew it wouldn't be long before the youth would have to go with the hunt, but he wasn't ready. There was so much more to it than met the eye; he talked to Rubama – it filled in details.

The persistence of a dry climate had aided the recovery of the grazing and browsing herds, and this was slowly affecting the savannah itself. The animals themselves, nibbling at saplings, would inhibit any tendency of the woodlands to re-establish and enlarge, and the activity benefited the grasslands. And that was fine by the people. With spoken language had come cooperation, and a fusion of enlightenment with cunning. Now, when they ventured onto the savannah it was with assuredness. Every aspect of the life cycles, habits, strengths and weaknesses of prey species was available to them, and with the tools they'd developed they could get more than just a meal from a carcase. Bone, horn and hide had qualities of interest to the inquisitive and enterprising mind;

hunting was occupying a much more prominent place among human aspirations.

More than ever before therefore, maturing youngsters had to scavenge and track down the knowledge which resided in their elders. Had they not done so, every advantage gained over countless generations would have withered away. There was only so much instruction they could take, though, and sooner or later youngsters had to find out at first hand.

Whereas early infancy had always been the time of greatest vulnerability, with the motivation to hunt intensifying, the inexperienced and sometimes uncoordinated adolescents - innocents in the front line – were vulnerable again, caught up in this accelerating rush to climb higher in the food-chain.

Rubama, utterly absorbed now in the scene unfolding before him, was at least showing promise – his rapt concentration as he observed and listened being a good sign. He'd achieved a perfectly adequate working vocabulary by the time he was five, and although his powers of comprehension might now be straining a little to fully understand the reasoning behind adult decisions, there was still enough plasticity in his system to take in expressions that Makwetu used which were new to him.

But there were challenges ahead – everybody sensed that, and he and his peer group were probably going to have to cajole yet more from the communication system they'd inherited – while there was still time.

~~~~~~~~
~~~~~~~~

And there was still time. In recent history it's been found that during periods when food is scarce for some sections of the population, their children grow to maturity much more slowly than those of well-fed classes. Is it possible that the *normal* slow rate at which human children grow today was established during those long, meagre millennia when the entire species was under stress? That evolution discovered an advantage in extending the timescale available for development? Such a scenario might help explain why language is able to go on growing even as youngsters approach maturity...

Either way, words themselves were amazingly flexible and adaptable, and Rubama and his friends would amass a great store of articulatory and linguistic manoeuvres to which they could apply meaning.[11] Their entire environment – people, animals, birds, insects, reptiles, plants, weather, landscape – had to be represented in its wealth of detail within the mind if they were to deal adequately with whatever occurred in the course of each day. But Rubama's group knew that at some future time they might each be much more active participants in protecting and organising their families and the clan, and to do this they would have to be deft communicators.

These were quite specific pressures for the youngsters. Being males, they would try their physical strength and do their best to get noticed, but while rash exploits might bring down swift criticism, bending the rules of language for their own private use carried no risk. It gave them a pleasing sense of their own identity, and allowed them freedom to test their communication to its limits. If they needed to let off social steam, speech was an ideal arena for them,[12] because while a fair proportion of what the youngsters said actually served no informative purpose at all, it could release energy and tension. Spoken language also had the valuable attribute of providing a possible substitute for violence, by channelling aggression and conflict through the wielding of words – discovering what utterances had power, on whom, when and why.

Nothing broke the link with the dark, wild places within, though, and words could provoke in more subversive ways than any pose, posture or act; they could twist and lodge in the memory, and sometimes the wounds they inflicted never healed.

But there was far more that was positive: the young could go on experimenting.[13] One ploy was to invent new words or phrases and use them, knowing older kin wouldn't understand – and this could cause great amusement. Within their group it was easy; they all knew the right context, and when something worked particularly well it would be absorbed into normal usage; it could even last long enough to become respectable, and be passed on to their own offspring - another small contribution to a living, evolving language.

Certainly, having their own style would further distinguish Rubama and his friends from the rest of the clan, enhancing their enjoyment and sense of confidence. Because if they were to survive, sometimes they felt the urge to hide their naivety beneath bravado, and reassure themselves that they really were going to be a force to be reckoned with.

In a sense what they were doing was revisiting the creative phase of infancy – playing with the sounds and sensations of speech – and coming up with adaptations of the existing system. It had strengthened their chances before and could do so again. Now, with the human lifestyle changing more rapidly than ever before, and gradually relying for their aids to survival on innovations in culture (the behaviours and abilities they passed across to one another[14]), the intimidating situation they were in acted as one more prompt – one last small spurt of growth. What differed, crucially, was that these young people were starting from a language base which was already extensive and complex. If they needed more from it to help them socially and practically, they couldn't ask the brain to expand any further – the skull had reached its limit. There wasn't room for each perception to have its own dedicated word, and so spoken language would have to rummage in its existing bag of tricks for a solution.

And one way was likely to have been the use of metaphor[15] - an apparently sophisticated feature of language based on the brain's ability to register similarities: it might start logically   with parts of the body, for example recognising the cliff 'face', the 'foot' of a hill, the 'mouth' of a stream. Then it could widen its scope: the sound of wavelets breaking along the shore of the lake and an animal lapping up the water might have been two entirely different events, but they sounded the same - so one word, 'lapping', could easily do for both. With its customary economy, spoken language recycled what was already understood and applied it in other situations; and as ever, once the context was 'grasped', so was the meaning.

In later years, metaphor would help describe emotional situations too. In a mood of unhappiness, Rubama might latch onto some recollection of a narrow valley's deep gloom, using the term to express his own; or when he noticed how the sun lit up a hillside - the bright side – he could take that for himself as well. Metaphor was a tool with endless possibilities. It, and the freedom to play fast and loose with any other features that might come in handy, provided spoken language with the flexibility it wanted to gradually cope with the highs and lows of fully modern adult existence.

But what about girls? Were they in a similar position to the young males – finding themselves somewhat daunted by what human society was expecting of them?

Maybe they were. The growing population was their responsibility – it was they who would produce the babies – a frightening thought if ever there was one. And because everyone was better fed, not only would women be capable of conceiving and delivering more babies, but they would be committed to the long-term upbringing of more of these children, because fewer would be lost to weakness or disease. On top of which, caring for the elderly members of families would be likely to fall to them. For if hunting and its associated activities took the men away more frequently or to somewhere distant, the life that revolved round the places used as a base would depend largely on the skills that women had.

For girls therefore, the age of puberty signalled much more than it had in earlier times and exploiting spoken language would be as vital a factor at this stage as it had been at the toddler stage. Like the boys, girls would find its current features were highly amenable to further expansion. In the creation and confines of a base, with its potential for hostility as well as harmony, communication would need to be finely tuned; to understand and respond to people effectively required delicacy.

Paradoxically, for both groups, spoken language was also an expression of the individual. It might have been the way someone talked which added a new dimension to the selection of a mate, or identified an ideal clan leader, invited respect, or generated dislike. Indeed, inside every person was a personality trying to get out. Spoken language came from within – it was the unique display of who that individual was. And somehow, the constraints of a system of auditory symbols, arranged in a form predetermined by how it had evolved, had to bridge the gap between what went on inside the mind and heart and what was presented outside. It was a tall order.

By the time this phase of their lives had been achieved, the spoken language of the up and coming generation had also reached its maturity. New vocabulary and expressions might go on being added, subtle meanings introduced by the use of intonation alone,[16] but all the mechanisms available were in place. Used proficiently, it would be central to the success of an ordered society.

~~~~~~~~

With Makwetu's careful help, Rubama joined the hunters and weathered the turbulent passage to manhood, and little Kigoma, now ten years old, had ample companions. But it had been in the thoughts of the clan's new leader for some time to strike out towards unexplored territories. Makwetu had become bent and old, and his feet hurt if he walked too far; so he had relinquished his role without
~~~~~~~~

bitterness, sensing a compelling mood for change approaching – and was relieved to know his responsibilities were over. The rhythm of the people's lives was bound in with that of the animal herds, always on the move, and some neighbouring populations had long gone where they led, north and beyond, an exodus which left its genetic tracks in those who came after.[17] But now the surge of restlessness was rising in the new clan.

So the talk was of possibilities. 'If we did that, what do you think we might find?   Look what happened last season…How should we prepare…?'

~~~~~~~~

Spoken language could allow thought to operate at a whole range of levels; it could cast the mind forward in imagination, backwards in recollection, it could be exquisitely lucid, or leave a question half asked, a sentence unfinished, and hesitations and silence could speak volumes. Adults, with their wealth of shared experiences sometimes only needed to utter a single word, spoken in a certain tone or accompanied by a look, and a great deal more could be assumed as understood. For them, language was so embedded that expression and comprehension would be taken for granted. It was easy to underestimate its limitations, though, and more often than not clarifications were called for.

~~~~~~~~

So the discussions continued until finally the clan was ready to gather its possessions and its children. Held at the breast, secured on the back with slings of hide or perched on the hip, the youngest would always be protected. Those children able to walk could travel alongside, observed and safeguarded through calls – so long as they understood and obeyed. If they didn't, the penalties were frighteningly swift; a flurry of huge talons and flapping wings could sweep up a straying infant with no chance of rescue. Such tragedies would emphasise the value of speech, and of attending to it.

But as the day for leaving had approached, it was clear that Makwetu would be staying behind. Conscious of the inevitable consequences of such a choice, Makwetu'a daughter grieved for him. Kigoma, saddened but less aware, would, throughout his life, remember the old man whenever the air freshened and the clan headed towards a lake, any lake, however small. His mind had made links, storing sensations as a reminder of the place and the person.

After they'd gone, Makwetu retreated to a rock shelter, shielded from the sun's rays by day and, so long as he could keep a fire burning, protected from animals and the cold at night. He comforted himself with an object his daughter had left, maybe forgotten, or more likely offered as a deliberate symbolic link between herself and the old man. He carried it with him along with his tools: an unfinished necklace of ostrich shell discs, shaped and smoothed and pierced. Makwetu had taken pleasure in Zina's talent. It was a startling new achievement – only the younger generations seemed to be able to make such things.

The necklace, falling at the last from the old man's fingers wasn't just a reminder to him of someone he loved; it was a rare and eloquent witness to what might have gone on in the human mind.

~~~~~~~~~

Aeons later, sifted from the hard floor of Enkapune Ya Muto Cave, it sheds light on the wearer.[18] Here was someone conscious of how she appeared, aware of the effect of adornment; here was a glimpse into a lifestyle – not always harsh and brutish – in which time could be devoted to making a thing of beauty. This wasn't a tool or a necessity. It had been fashioned with care to please the eye and to give enjoyment.

And crucial to it all, the evidence of how intricate the workings of the brain had become: pieces of an ostrich eggshell could be imagined into a totally different role. The brain directed their modification, reshaping, matching, then linking into a sequence. By using sinew the whole acquired a structure, and the result could express something about the woman herself.

In a sense this might support the notion that the capacity really had existed for spoken language to develop the kind of complexity suggested in this story, because it too had emerged through a similar process: modifying sounds, matching them, linking them into sequences and creating a structure for them. Above all, it allowed us to communicate something about ourselves to each other.

Over its lengthy history, beginning with our pre-human ancestors, communication has been with us in some form, adapting with us all the way. Of course, other animal species weathered the storms and seasons too, but our successive species alone hit upon vocal communication as the system that
~~~~~~~~~

would ultimately go to extremes on their behalf. Spoken language had grown up with them – its relationship was symbiotic, dependent as much on them as they on it – and as its attributes permeated into intellectual activities people would realise that in an *un*spoken form it was giving them the gift of conscious thought.

Spoken language had behaved rather like a vine in the way it had intertwined itself through the life of both the individual and his society. Or perhaps it resembled a great forest tree in which, at various levels, a multitude of different activities could take place. People might well stand in awe of such an amazing organism.

But they might also easily overlook how it had all begun, forgetting the smallness of its seed.

The seedbed for spoken language…

- As populations recovered, vocabularies changed and expanded through contact with non-local speakers.

- Lifestyles changed again, and the long period necessary to reach maturity allowed further language features to be added.

- Prior to the rigours of adulthood, young modern humans reacted to these pressures by demanding more from spoken language, experimenting with its existing forms.

- There were limits to brain growth, but language circumvented this by the use of metaphor, structure and intonation only.

EPILOGUE

There are just a few more things.

Apologies
For obvious reasons it was necessary to use present-day English in the dialogues of this story. It's been a huge drawback, if only because it has failed to convey the richness of the repertoire of sounds our hominin forbears bequeathed to us. Other languages use clicks, and tricks of the tongue that trap and expel air in ways that often, for English speakers, defy imitation; and people can use infinitesimal variations in the placement of tongue and shape of lips, or introduce changes in vocal pitch – the tonal languages – to give the languages and dialects of the world their special and treasured characteristics.

Another difficulty has been that current English has also had to represent, on behalf of ancestral humans, equivalent meanings through its own particular combinations of sounds, syllables and words, and comparable structures through its own particular grammar – all of which have obscured the diversity of expressive devices that have come, gone and exist in spoken languages.

Worse still, inflexible print has bestowed permanence on what were (and still are) ephemeral strings of sounds borne on the breath. In its rigidity, each separated word has obscured how fluid and holistic the expression and understanding of vocal communication was (and still is.) The written word will have influenced how we think about spoken language – we can visualise something our ancestors only heard.

Given the time-lapse, therefore, even attempting such a task could have seemed absurd. Yet the scenarios in which all those ancestral humans adapted and pushed out the boundaries of their communication system needed the sound of their voices. The infants and adults were in real-life situations – they wouldn't have kept quiet! Using English was the only option, and apologies are offered to the reader for any discomfort felt.

None of this, however, precludes curiosity about how our predecessors really sounded. And if they were indeed using spoken language in the way this story suggests, could anything remain from its pioneering days? Given its fluidity, its transience and tantalising refusal to linger around old bones, that seems highly unlikely.

And yet...

Whispers from the past
There's the curious coincidence of the name of Africa itself – *Afriqiyya* or *Ifriqiyya*.[1] The root of this word is *firq* and its meaning is 'dividing', 'separating', or 'showing difference'. Could the first two meanings be a trace of the recognition the first fully modern humans had that they were indeed dividing themselves – as some clans chose to stay while others moved on, migrating away from the continent which had cradled them? Or was it their adventurous exodus to Arabia, crossing the mouth of the Red Sea when the sea level fell low enough for them to pick their way from reef to reef? Contemplating the hazards for however long it took, plucking up courage, imprinting what they saw on their inner map – here was a barrier physically separating them from whatever lay ahead and what remained behind. And the third meaning –

'showing difference'? If their restless groups paused to recount their stories, was this the name they gave to some memory of their old home? As new landscapes spread before them and they acclimatised, how else would they explain their origins to curious children and grandchildren, except by a passed-on recollection of somewhere very different?

There is too a very slender possibility that some basic vocabulary may even now be detectable in certain words, one which has similarities in both root sounds and meanings. It overlaps the distinctions between many of the seventeen language families which have been proposed as ancestral to all those spoken in the world today.[2]

It would be as though the words went with the people as they migrated, like legacies from a very distant past. Across the language groups, from Africa to Asia, America and even aboriginal Australia, some sound combinations are consistently recognised as indicating broadly related things. They include such words as these: *k'olo* - 'hole' in English, 'hole' or 'crack' in Finnish, *kul* – 'cave' in Korean.

There's *puti* meaning vulva - 'vulva' in Tulu (in the Dravidian or Indian family of languages), *putain* – 'whore' in modern French, *pot* – 'vulva' in Hebrew.

And *tik* - 'finger' or 'one', from Greenland to New Guinea, 'finger' or 'hand' in Karok, one of the Amerind languages, *tek* – 'fingernail' in Boven Mbian, an Indo-Pacific language; it's there in the Latin, *dig (-itus)* – 'finger', and of course, we find it in 'tickle'.

Other words touch on more primal concerns, and they too similarly transcend today's language barriers – *mano,* used for 'man' or 'people', *kuna* meaning 'woman' or 'mother' (found in our 'queen'), and *mako*, meaning 'child' or 'son'. And *aq'wa*, 'water', that fundamental necessity of everyone's life.

But the idea that these words are relics of a proto-language isn't widely accepted, so what else could explain such coincidences?

Well, there's sound symbolism (or synaesthesia – a mixing of the senses). It seemed reasonable to suppose that early on, our ancestors would re-enact the sounds they heard in nature as accurately as they could, in order to identify specific creatures to each other. Perhaps this mechanism extended itself to other sensory experiences, such as the things they saw (as suggested in Chapter 6). After all, the central nervous system of the brain processes both incoming and outgoing data – it would be surprising if the one didn't make some impression on the other in passing.

As a common internal mechanism, therefore, this sound symbolism would behave in the same way for everyone, so that at a certain early level, the particular qualities or characteristics of objects might be expressed using the same kinds of speech sounds – whatever the geographical location of the speaker.

This doesn't tell us whether the words in question are ancient, however.

Unless we look once more at very small children. To them the 'feel' of words, the sound of them, and their meaning, are inseparable from the objects themselves. It would have been the same for our ancestors as they first began expressing themselves using phonemes (units of sound capable of conveying meaning) as a response to their environment. There may therefore be a clue to the antiquity of that basic vocabulary in how the words are put together.

Almost all of the expressions quoted above are composed of syllables each with a consonant and a vowel. No clusters such as 'scr' or 'spl', not even blends: 'bl', 'fr' or 'sw', and no polysyllables – they are two syllables long, just like the earliest words of children. Yet these words, for all their ease of utterance, aren't the typical vocabulary of infants, lingering into adulthood. They speak of adult concerns.

As such, are they suggesting an origin dating back to a phase when mature articulation was that limited? Any resonance from a very ancient past would surely have to reflect the neuro-muscular capabilities required to make the sounds, and early on these might have had more in common with the simply-shaped calls of animals than with the intricate phonology, or sound systems of human speech into which they developed. For in the same way that animals are identified by their calls wherever they are found, our pre-human calls too must have been characteristic of our species, over time and even place.

Walking and Talking
Throughout this attempt to trace the emergence of spoken language in ancestral humans, it has seemed impossible to separate its advance from the sequential seeking after habitable places which would have been their way of life. However long the time-scale involved, at every step of the way their adaptations used what brain and body could already do – and pushed them a little further. They *had* to cope with the climate and the environment in which they found themselves, and as the brain's

expanding functions tackled the demands of every day, communication was affected too. Vocal expression wasn't an independent, separate module, it was an integral part of an individual's response to his situation. As it broadened its scope – whether in the comprehension of the utterances of others, or in shaping patterns of self-expression – it gleaned facilities from its cognitive companions, even if, at first glance they might seem remote from the sounds of speech and the structuring of language.

We've certainly come a long way, in many senses, but for all the present sophistication of spoken language - its ability to range from the mundane to the magnificent almost in the same breath - even now we aren't completely unique in some aspects of our communication. These are detectable in our chimpanzee cousins: facial expression, posture, arm gestures and intonation, and we might well have shared these with them when our two lineages diverged, between eight and five million years ago.

So these features came with us when our ancient predecessors left the trees and began to walk. But things would never be the same again. While it was adult imperatives that determined how lifestyles changed, it was the young who gradually became more vulnerable. It was their adaptive capacities that delivered solutions for them, at every stage transforming their calls in ways that made survival (and survival to breed) just a little more likely.

To support this view I've drawn on information about the forerunners which prompt the growth of spoken language today, and the essential dynamic interplay of factors needed to turn infants' earliest cries into competent linguistic communication. Most children develop these skills so easily that the processes go unrecognised, and it's only when a child has difficulties that their importance becomes apparent. At its most stark, spoken language will not develop normally without them; the rare cases of feral children[3] are a heart-breaking illustration of that.

By a similar token, without such processes occurring in the infants of ancestral species, how else would their calls have become spoken language?

Mature spoken language, in all its complexity and variety, has traditionally been the main focus of attention in seeking to understand its evolution, but small children have quite a story to tell too.

Lastly…
As for the adult imperatives which (in slightly more recent times) impinged on my own childhood – how to ensure I survived, despite WW2 and its aftermath – these demanded very little in the way of adaptation. So no ground-breaking evolutionary innovations there. But like generations before me I was protected and nurtured, and in an era with few toys, took great delight in the sounds of words, the stories told round a glowing coal fire, and what excitement could be found in the countryside. It was a quieter time, too – no TV, limited radio programmes, few household appliances, no music in shops, little traffic noise. Listening while people talked was easy.

Happily I now have grandchildren of my own, and the woodlands we walk in are quiet, bright with beech and birch, typical of the Danish landscape where they live.

Like many children around the world, they are growing up at ease in more than one language, and their abilities astonish me, even though I do have an inkling about how they do it.

Sometimes in the forest tree roots make the paths uneven, and when they were very small the children would occasionally stumble and fall. Then their mother would put her arms round them, rocking gently to comfort them.

"*Så*," she'd say, "ssaahh", and the sound was soothing, like the breeze as it rustled through the leaves of the trees.

APPENDIX 1

Notes about how today's children develop spoken language.

'Survival of the Smallest' has suggested how primate communication might have evolved to become the system we call human spoken language. It proposes that it was the young who were the driving force, as they reacted to the effects of changes in adult lifestyles.

In order to show why it seemed reasonable to draw such scenarios for our predecessors - even across so great a timescale – the following notes are provided in parallel with the book's chapters. They give brief glimpses of comparable processes of spoken language development in today's children, showing the emergence of particular features and the influences which foster their growth.

Then as now, an inner motivation to communicate changing needs would spark an interplay between infants and their carers, and this would combine with their physical, cognitive and social experiences to prompt new skills. Little by little, then as now, vocal communication would accumulate components – both in the understanding and use of expressive speech – that would grow to serve each individual in his own time and place.

Today's infants and children advance from simple cries to competent spoken language against the background of a modern world, but the dynamics underpinning the communicative efforts of our ancient ancestors may nevertheless have emerged through circumstances which we would broadly recognise.

[These notes are not referenced, but the following two books are highly recommended in their entirety: Baby Talk, Maximise your child's potential in just 30 minutes a day, by Dr. Sally Ward, and Listen to your Child, a Parent's Guide to Children's Language by David Crystal. These show in detail how spoken language emerges and what conditions, activities and approaches contribute to its development.]

CHAPTER 1

Babies exploit the use of their voice from the moment of birth – it is all they can do to <u>attract attention.</u> Their parents and carers meet their needs by <u>responding</u> to their cries, trying to work out what's wrong, and many use a baby monitor to ensure they can hear. Crying is obviously a survival mechanism for the baby, and the pattern of this simple interaction signals the importance of <u>vocal communication</u> between them.
In all cultures babies are <u>moved</u> or rocked and this is important because the motion both calms them and helps in their <u>neurological</u> development - a vital feature if they are to achieve the fine physical <u>coordination</u> needed for spoken language.

CHAPTER 2

The change to solid food exercises babies' speech musculature as they encounter new tastes and textures, and they babble and gurgle after feeds. They <u>hear</u> their own <u>sounds</u>, and are interested when people talk to them – they are absorbing the different acoustic qualities which characterise speech sounds. <u>Listening</u> is obviously a vital factor underpinning all the developments which follow, and babies today need an environment in which this happens easily. They benefit from an approach from carers which helps them to <u>focus </u>on what they hear. It takes a long time for their <u>attention span</u> to grow, and they are easily distracted, but their ability to understand and use speech will depend on having good listening habits right from the start.
Everyday sounds, such as a door closing or bathwater running, will already have <u>significance</u> for babies, and this paves the way for attaching 'meaning' to vocal sounds.
From early on they will have been seeking to make <u>eye contact </u>with those closest to them, and as they begin to play this will often involve imitating some simple actions that they see. Because copying is such a two-way process, encouragement to copy speech sounds arises when babies hear their own sounds repeated back to them.

As they become more aware of those around them, infants enjoy the interest they attract when they say simple syllables. And when their carers <u>repeat</u> the names of important people and things, making them stand out, infants recognise that there are different <u>meanings</u> in particular groups of speech sounds.

Then, when certain syllables they say obviously result in getting them something they want (bi-ckie, te-ddy) they will be highly <u>motivated</u> to try others, and their earlier strings of babble are replaced by more purposeful vocalisations. At this stage they enjoy it when those around copy a simple gesture or action, and play <u>turn-taking</u> games, and in this they are already using the same give-and-take principle which will underlie conversation.

It is vital that background sounds (TV, music etc.) are kept to a minimum, so that the importance and pleasure of talking comes across to them.

Infants reach to touch things, exploring with their fingers, and they readily use their <u>hands</u> to point and wave bye-bye. Doing this helps them <u>communicate</u> what they can't yet say. Adults use <u>facial expression</u>, gestures and <u>signs</u> as well as intonation and speech to communicate with each other, and using these features clearly to infants makes it easier for them to <u>understand</u> what's said to them. They show by their actions and reactions that they understand a lot more than they are able to say, and it's a boost to infants when their carers <u>accept</u> their signs and vocal efforts, saying the infants' "target" words back to them.

Vocal activity – their own and that of their carers – is a source of <u>enjoyment</u> for infants, and they are already familiar with the rhythms and variations of sounds that are the characteristic features of their own language.

CHAPTER 5

As children become more mobile their <u>curiosity</u> about their surroundings helps to drive their communication. They need (and thrive on) the <u>social interactions</u> made possible and enhanced by their growing understanding and <u>use</u> of speech. <u>Songs, music and rhymes</u> support and foster this growth.

Children progress when they realise that <u>words</u> can '<u>stand for</u>' things that are familiar in their environment – even when they can't see them. (They may crawl over to a toy box if asked 'Where's your tractor?') They show their grasp of the <u>usefulness</u> of words when they stretch them to try and cope with something new that they've seen - e.g. 'doggie' for other animals as well. The continued realisation that spoken language achieves things for them prompts more experiments; it is becoming a tool for finding out as well as expressing need.

Children's physical development gradually allows them to engage in yet more activities and to widen their experiences. They build up a <u>'core'</u> of useful words (similar in meaning the world over) which help them to <u>affect</u> what happens to them. Crucially, the more they understand what's said to them the better they get at using their own speech. And when those around make simple comments that <u>match</u> what children are <u>experiencing,</u> and what they might want to say, they absorb the fact that short phrases (<u>linked</u> <u>words)</u> can help them express themselves more effectively - 'teddy-gone', 'more-bickie'. When carers share in the pleasure of saying these phrases (by repeating them) it contributes to getting them established. Similarly, when there's a problem, the simplest comments that help to soothe - e.g. 'aah, poor finger...' 'poor knee' – demonstrate how these longer utterances work.

CHAPTER 7

With increasing confidence, children want to engage with people and get <u>involved</u> in whatever's going on, often shouting with excitement. But their efforts to express this interest by <u>commenting,</u> telling or <u>asking</u> are sometimes difficult to understand, especially to those outside the close family circle. They are using their spoken language to explore, and aren't sure how to put their thoughts into words. A valuable interplay arises when those around keep trying with suggestions until they hit on a phrase that matches the intention, and <u>say it back</u>.
Often, too, the problem is due to children finding some sounds difficult to say; <u>coordinating</u> the physical acts necessary for speech is a complex process. It helps children when people take care that they <u>hear</u> their <u>words</u> said <u>clearly</u> back, without correction or being urged to copy. They make progress when their surroundings make it easy for them to <u>listen</u> – and when they feel comfortable communicating through speech.
Gradually what children say will move towards adult expectations and be more comprehensible.

CHAPTER 8

When children begin to be aware that certain kinds of things around them share some similarities – that they can be <u>classified</u> - building vocabulary in our word-rich world becomes much more manageable. Experiences during daily life which demonstrate this organisation are helpful – e.g. cats and dogs are different but still animals; bananas and apples are different but still fruit. So games which also foster this cognitive process, such as <u>matching</u> and <u>grouping</u>, contribute to spoken language in the same way.
The brain needs words themselves to be categorised according to how they operate, if they are to <u>link</u> themselves together in productive ways. Carers can make this easier if they show how usefully particular <u>kinds of words</u> collaborate: verbs and objects – 'throw ball', people and objects - 'Daddy's shoe', adjectives and people – 'good girl!' Telling children <u>about</u> things makes a difference too – they can often say what something <u>is</u>, but their language grows when they know what people are <u>doing</u>, can point to a <u>big</u> or <u>little</u> object, or be asked to put a toy <u>on</u> or <u>in</u> a box. Children enjoy <u>showing</u> they've understood such things, without pressure to tell. Listening continues to be vital.

CHAPTER 9

The routines and events of daily life provide natural opportunities for children to absorb and remember the way things happen – their order, or <u>sequence</u>. This is important in itself, but also in paving the way for children to cope when longer sentences are said to them, and in nudging them towards using the order of words that is typical of their own language. As they experience new things, their spontaneous efforts can 'map onto' this essential supporting framework for spoken language - the <u>beginnings of grammar</u>. It helps them when carers take what they've said then 'recast' it as a model, showing how adding another word can encapsulate what's happened, fostering an <u>expansion</u> from two to <u>three-word phrases</u>.
The same technique works if children miss off <u>sounds,</u> or confuse one with another – they may begin to notice a sound at the beginning or end of a word if it's emphasised for them, or pick up more precisely on how it's pronounced. Any activities which encourage <u>attentive listening</u> will contribute to both these aspects of spoken language.

CHAPTER 10

From playing alongside others, children gradually mature to discover the fun of playing <u>with</u> others. They use the <u>richer vocabulary</u> at their command, and make it work for them by supplying and stringing together enough 'bits' of information to get their friends to do as they say – or state their own response to what they're told to do! <u>Listening</u> and <u>understanding</u> when their carers explain simply their plans for outings, or just what they're going to do next shows another role for spoken language: how it can reflect something that could happen in the <u>future</u> – away from the here-and-now. Given the opportunities, children will make the most of their language to <u>influence</u> those around them, and exert some control over events which will affect them.

CHAPTER 11

Language development doesn't progress in a linear fashion; stages overlap and features emerge which may be fostered in different ways as children grow. So their on-going <u>interest</u> in what adults and older children are doing is always a rich source of experience at any level. Carers can really deepen children's <u>understanding</u> – and their <u>self-expression</u> – by noticing what has caught their <u>attention.</u> Talking about such things, (rather than trying to direct them onto something else, however 'educational') really helps to satisfy their hunger for finding out. But the information has to come in suitable <u>'chunks'</u> – small enough for them to 'digest'.

Children's language development also requires carers to respond to the endless <u>questions</u> – even if it does mean saying the same thing over and over again; it is by this means that children become familiar with the typical question and answer patterns we use.

CHAPTER 12

Many children master articulation gradually, finding it difficult to make some sounds and clusters of sounds until their lips and tongue become sufficiently <u>agile.</u> The <u>habit of careful listening</u> continues to pay off, and also enables them to understand the <u>longer</u> and more involved sentences that people will use around them as they get older. They also get better at remembering things they've heard.

As their own self-expression becomes easier however, they really gain <u>confidence</u> by having opportunities to listen and talk to people <u>beyond</u> their familiar circle. They gain an increasing awareness of the <u>wide range</u> of ways in which spoken language is used.

CHAPTER 13

Just as children explore the physical, material world around them, making sense of it through their understanding and use of spoken language, so too they need to be able to make sense of the world of human relationships.

From the start children have experienced sudden feelings and deep emotions, and as their social opportunities widen, they need to be able to recognize how others feel too, reflecting that sensitivity in the way they communicate with them. Carers foster these skills by making sure their own facial expressions illustrate their reactions truthfully, and their voices and words match too – praise and pleasure clearly contrasting with warning or disapproval. It isn't easy for children to tell what's going on in someone's mind.

Even today small children may be excluded from certain places if their behaviour is thought likely to be disruptive, so helping them understand what is acceptable to other people improves their prospects of being liked and welcomed in the company of others.

As children try to get to grips with the complexities of the situations and interactions in which they're involved, they want to find out why things happen. Given plenty of opportunities to hear explanations (repeated as required), children's own spontaneous spoken language begins to show evidence that they're eager to use a more adult style of language. They're discovering for themselves the underlying rules of grammar which support longer more mature self-expression. They aren't simply copying, and this shows when they don't know the exceptions, e.g. - 'we wented shopping.'

They have enough skill now to be creative in what they say – to convey shades of meaning, and their own individual perceptions of life.

Although they may be more capable of managing the intricate arrangements of speech sounds which allow them to do all this, they may still struggle to be as fluent as older speakers; patient accepting listeners will normally see this phase fade away.

Children derive enormous pleasure from the act of talking – they're often amused by how words and phrases feel and sound, and may seem to talk just for the sake of talking.

They enjoy games, songs and stories with repeated refrains – 'rituals' – and like to go over and over special outings or events. These activities help them increase their ability to remember the typical forms of phrases and sentences, and introduce them to a more adult style of communicating. By hearing and copying good patterns of spoken language, children become adept at using longer and more complicated expressions, something which then filters into their own spontaneous conversations. This kind of deliberate repetition also provides them with a valuable technique for learning, which they can use to help commit new knowledge to memory.

CHAPTER 15

Late childhood and adolescence see further growth in spoken language as emotional, <u>educational</u>, social and <u>cultural</u> <u>demands</u> exert their pressure. Youngsters continue to discover effective ways of communicating, particularly within their peer group, and they test and adapt features of spoken language to serve their own ends. There may be a contrast between the style of speech used amongst themselves and that used with adults, reflecting the increasing self-awareness which develops at this time.

Opportunities to <u>experience</u> the wide breadth of its <u>functions</u>, the scope of its <u>power</u> and the <u>richness</u> of its forms are vital preparations for whatever life has in store for them.

APPENDIX 2

Swahili names used in the story.

NAME	MEANING
Maneno -	Words
Tatu -	Three
Hami -	Defend
Kifimbo -	Stick
Nuru -	Light
Badru -	Full Moon
Pili -	Second
Nyuni -	Bird
Tumbo -	Stomach
Hurani -	Restive
Hiba -	Gift
Kipanga -	Falcon
Ducha -	Little
Chiku -	Chatterer
Makwetu -	Our Place

Zina -   Beauty

Kigoma -   Small Drum

Kitunda -   Small Fruit

Rubama -   Possibility

REFERENCES AND NOTES

INTRODUCTION
1. Klein, R. The Human Career. The University of Chicago Press, 1999. pp.248 - 249. How climate change and its consequences on forests led to bipedalism as an adaptation.

2 Goodall, J. The Chimpanzees of Gombe. The Belknap Press of Harvard University, 1986. p.127. Chimpanzee calls – descriptions, and the feelings and emotions with which they are associated. The chimpanzee communication system has been taken as the primate model capable of giving rise to the precursors of human speech and language. This approach may be justified by the close genetic similarity between the two species.

3. Morgan, E. The Descent of the Child. Souvenir Press Ltd. 1994. p.135. Language - a skill acquired by children, not adults.

4. Deacon, T. The Symbolic Species. The Penguin Press, 1997. p.123, 135 and 205. The appropriateness of children's neural set-up for language acquisition.

5. Aitchison, J. The Seeds of Speech. Cambridge University Press, 2000. p.31 and 35. The time-frame and method through which language acquisition is achieved.

6. Ward, S. An Investigation into the Effectiveness of an Early Intervention Method for Delayed Language Development in Young Children, in the International Journal of Language and Communication Disorders, 1999, Vol.34, no. 3. p.244. Quoting Lennenberg (1967), whose premise on language acquisition recognises the association of biological programming with environmental stimuli, which is a feature of both language and much animal behaviour.

7. Goodall, J. The Chimpanzees of Gombe. The Belknap Press, 1986. p.265. The likelihood of young chimpanzees being responsible for the introduction of new feeding behaviours – citing the example of infant and juvenile Japanese macaques.

8. Christiansen, M. and Kirby, S. Language Evolution. Oxford University Press, 2005. A definitive anthology of 17 papers from the widest range of disciplines.

9. Atkinson, Q. Report in the journal Science, 15/4/11, describing studies on phonemic diversity which support the view that the languages of the world are descended from a single ancestral language originating in Africa.

10. Klein, R. The Human Career. The University of Chicago Press, 1999. pp.4-7. A description of the forces which bring about evolutionary change.

Further Sources.

Bee, H. The Developing Child. Addison-Wesley Educational Publishers, 1977. p.12 quoting Greenfield, P. 1994, and p.311, quoting Tronick, Morelli & Ivey 1992. Also Ochs, E. Rethinking Context. Cambridge University Press, 1992, p.335. All describing alternative cultural approaches to child nurturing. Also p101. The plasticity of infant neural systems.

Downer, J. Supersense. BBC Books, 1988. p.68. The workings of the human ear and (p85) ultrasonic communication in rodents.

Diamond, J. The Rise and Fall of the Third Chimpanzee. Vintage Press, 1991. p137. The problem of the gulf between animal vocalisations and human language.

Finch, G. How to Study Linguistics. Palgrave, Macmillan, 2003. pp.85-107 Analysing spoken language.

Gibson, K. and Ingold, T. Tools, Language and Cognition in Human Evolution. Cambridge University Press, 1993. p.14. The value of (childhood) developmental studies in understanding the mastery of tasks which are precursors of spoken language.

Goldin-Meadow, S. When does Gesture become Language? in Gibson, K, and Ingold, T. Tools, Language and Cognition in Human Evolution. Cambridge University Press, 1993. pp.63-85. A study of gesture used as a primary communication system by deaf children of hearing parents.

Morgan, E. The Descent of the Child. Souvenir Press Ltd. 1994. p. viii In relation to evolutionary change, how animal behaviour responds to what has happened, not what's going to happen.

Oates, J & Grayson, A. Cognitive and Language Development in Children. Blackwell Publishing Ltd, 2004. p14. The interactive nature of infant brain development, with particular reference to the development of spoken language.

Ward, S. An Investigation into the Effectiveness of an Early Intervention Method for Delayed Language Development in Young Children, in the International Journal of Language and Communication Disorders, 1999, Vol.34, no. 3, pp.243-244 Implications of delay in language development. Also Ward, S. Baby Talk. Arrow Books, 2004. pp.12-14 The stimulus to an infant's language of the intellectual developments which arise out of exploration of his environment.

Winston, R. Human Instinct. Bantam Books. 2002. pp.17-36. The possible influence of our evolutionary past on present day behaviours.

CHAPTER 1
1. Klein, R. The Human Career. The University of Chicago Press, 1999. This book is the main source for data on all hominin species.
2. Merenstein, G. & Gardner, S. Handbook of Neonatal Intensive Care. Mosby, St Louis, 1993. p.589. Also Morrison, D., Pothier, P. & Horr, K. Sensory-Motor Dysfunction and Therapy in Infancy and Early Childhood. Charles C. Thomas, Springfield, 1978, p.79. Descriptions of the effect of touching and moving very young babies in order to stimulate specific aspects of brain growth.
3. Klein, R. The Human Career. The University of Chicago Press, 1999. p.169. The footprints at Laetoli. A fuller description can be found on the following website:
http://www.humanorigins.si.edu/evidence/behavior/laetoli-footprint-trails

CHAPTER 2
1. Goodall, J. The Chimpanzees of Gombe. Cambridge, Mass. The Belknap Press of Harvard University, 1986. Fig. 6.2, p.127. Chimpanzee calls and the emotions or feelings with which they are associated.
2. Ward, S. Baby Talk. Arrow Books, 2004. p.54. Sharing a focus of attention. Also Hurford, J. The Language Mosaic in Christiansen, M. and Kirby, S. Language Evolution, Oxford University Press, 2003. p. 47. Primate ability to establish joint attention.

3. Studdert-Kennedy, M. and Goldstein, L. The Gestural Origin of Discrete Infinity, in Christiansen, M. and Kirby, S. Language Evolution, Oxford University Press, 2003. pp 239-240. The movements involved in feeding as the basis for the motor component of speech.

4. Klein, R. The Human Career. The University of Chicago Press, 1999. Fig 4.16, p.193 Changes in the nature of mastication from *Australopithecus afarensis* onwards.

5. Crowe, I. The Quest for Food. Tempus Publishing, Ltd, 2000. p.31. The wider diet available as the landscape became more open.

6. Cooke, J. and Williams, D. Working with Children's Language. Winslow Press, 1991. p.9. The importance of feeding in strengthening the muscles an infant uses during speech.

7. Snowdon, C. A Comparative Approach to Language Parallels in Gibson, K. and Ingold, T. Tools, Language and Cognition in Human Evolution. Cambridge University Press, 1993. pp.116-118, quoting Marler. A discussion of the pressures for an extended period of vocal learning in migratory bird populations, and the suggestion that while primates remained sedentary there would have been no selective pressure for a longer learning period.

8. Snowdon, C. A Comparative Approach to Language Parallels in Gibson, K, and Ingold, T. Tools, Language and Cognition in Human Evolution. Cambridge University Press, 1993. p.116. Studies of vervet monkeys (Seyfarth and Cheyney, 1986) show them using calls which differentiate between aerial and ground predators.

9. Winston, R. Human Instinct. Bantam Books. 2002. pp.356-358. Description of the research relating to mirror neurones in humans, and their possible relevance to communication. Also Arbib, M. The Evolving Mirror System in Christiansen, M. and Kirby, S. Language Evolution, Oxford university Press, 2005. pp 190-194. More detailed discussion of the Mirror System Hypothesis and its relevance to language readiness.

10. Crowe, I. The Quest for Food. Tempus Publishing, Ltd, 2000. p.32. The observation that chimpanzees living in more open habitats tend to exploit a wider range of food resources, including eggs.

11. Klein, R. The Human Career. The University of Chicago Press, 1999. p.174. Geological changes in the Lake Turkana Basin between 4 and 2 million years ago.

12. Deacon, T. The Symbolic Species. The Penguin Press, 1997. p.298. The relationship between the ape 'brain plan' and language.

13. Deacon, T. The Symbolic Species. The Penguin Press, 1997. pp.194-195. The growth of brain cells, how they make connections and organise their function of information processing.

CHAPTER 3

1.Klein, R. The Human Career. The University of Chicago Press, 1999. pp.251-252. Climate fluctuations between 2 and 3 million years ago.

2. Klein, R. The Human Career. The University of Chicago Press, 1999. p.220. Provisional description of *Homo habilis*.

3. Aitchison, J. The Seeds of Speech. Cambridge University Press, 2000. p.84. Primate lip smacks and tongue tip sounds. Also Lieberman, P. Motor Control, Speech, and Evolution, in Christiansen, M. and Kirby, S. Language Evolution, Oxford university Press, 2005. p258. Consonants and vowels considered possible in chimpanzee vocalisations.

4. **Hurford, J.** The Language Mosaic in Christiansen, M. and Kirby, S. Language Evolution, Oxford University Press, 2003. p48. The earliest use of a particular utterance standing for something – to show personal identity.

5. **The Guardian** website: www.theguardian.com/science/2013/apr/27/aquatic-ape-theory-primate-evolution .

6. **Morgan, E.** The Descent of the Child. Souvenir Press Ltd. 1994. p. 165, quoting Eisenberg, J. 1981. The descended larynx and presence of voluntary breath control in aquatic birds and mammals in contrast to terrestrial ones.

7. **Morgan, E.** The Descent of the Child. Souvenir Press Ltd. 1994. p.135. The wider sound repertoire of infants compared to adults.

8. **Ward, S.** Baby Talk. Arrow Books, 2004. p.52. The pleasures of babbling.

9. **Finch, G.** How to Study Linguistics. Palgrave Macmillan, 2003. p.22. The social usefulness of 'semantically empty' language. (Quoting Berne, E. in Games People Play, 1968.)

10. **Deacon, T.** The Symbolic Species. The Penguin Press, 1997. p.383. The importance of communicative behaviours to mate selection.

CHAPTER 4

1. **Deacon, T.** The Symbolic Species. The Penguin Press, 1997. p.251. Human vocal skills at 2 million years ago.

2. **Leakey, R.** The Origin of Humankind. Wedenfield & Nicolson. London, 1994. pp.46-48

Implications for ancestral humans, especially newborns, of an enlarging cranial volume.

3. Ward, S. Baby Talk. Arrow Books, 2004. p.40. The baby's sensitivity to the broad sound features of human speech.

4. Crystal, D. Listen to Your Child. Penguin Books, 1986. p.40. The infant's increasing muscular control over his vocal organs.

5. Oates, J & Grayson, A. Cognitive and Language Development in Children. Blackwell Publishing Ltd, 2004. p81. The progressive stages in infants' vocal activity as they move from the simplest sound–making, through play and experimentation to particular forms of babbling.

6. Ward, S. Baby Talk. Arrow Books, 2004. p.47. Understanding the emotional content of language.

7. Ward, S. Baby Talk. Arrow Books, 2004. p.40. The resonating capability of the infant ear.

8.Oates, J & Grayson, A. Cognitive and Language Development in Children. Blackwell Publishing Ltd, 2004. p.91 The value to infants of hearing specific words consistently used, and issues relating to context.

9. Ward, S. Baby Talk. Arrow Books, 2004. pp.78-79. The relationship between attention control and understanding.

10. Aitchison, J. The Seeds of Speech. Cambridge University Press, 2000. p.72. The distinction between gestures and signs: "signs" are conscious/voluntary, "gestures" are involuntary.

11. Diamond, J. The Rise and Fall of the Third Chimpanzee. Vintage Press, 1991. p.47. The (inevitable) absence of evidence for the existence of fine neural modifications in fossil skulls.

12. Morgan, E. The Descent of the Child. Souvenir Press Ltd. 1994. p.122. Vocal activity for an infant's immediate use, not for when he becomes an adult.

13. Klein, R. The Human Career. The University of Chicago Press, 1999. p.234 and Fig 4.40, p.235. The (Oldowan) tools made and used by *Homo habilis*.

14. Klein, R. The Human Career. The University of Chicago Press, 1999. pp. 239-240. Interpreting the finds at Koobi Fora.

15. Pinker, S. The Language Instinct. The Penguin Press. 1994. pp.300-307. The lateralisation of the brain in relation to spoken language.

CHAPTER 5

1. Klein, R. The Human Career. The University of Chicago Press, 1999. p.174. Geological changes in the Lake Turkana Basin between 4 and 2 million years ago.

2. Klein, R. The Human Career. The University of Chicago Press, 1999. p.250. Adaptations to heat in *Homo ergaster*.

3. Crowe, I. The Quest for Food. Tempus Publishing, Ltd, 2000. p.32 and 41. Water as a factor in where hominids went and what they might eat.

4. Klein, R. The Human Career. The University of Chicago Press, 1999. pp.252-253. Behavioural changes in response to a terrestrial lifestyle and longer postnatal dependency in infants.

5. Winston, R. Human Instinct. Bantam Books. 2002. p.84. The power of in infant's cry.

6. Aitchison, J. The Seeds of Speech. Cambridge University Press, 2000. p.80. Pitch frequencies of human speech, and the pre-existence of the capacity to hear them.

7. Aitchison, J. The Seeds of Speech. Cambridge University Press, 2000. p.123. Suggested early human vocabulary. Also Crystal, D. Listen to Your Child. Penguin Books, 1986. pp.68-69. The typical infant vocabulary during the second year.

8. Winston, R. Human Instinct. Bantam Books, 2002. pp.161-163. Suggestions regarding male/female roles in ancestral humans.

9. Stoppard, M. Complete Baby and Child Care. Dorling Kindersley, 1995. p. 200. Girls acquire language more readily than boys. Also Morgan, E. The Descent of the Child. Souvenir Press Ltd. 1994. p.135. The mother/infant relationship as a reason for girls talking earlier than boys.

10. Ward, S. Baby Talk. Arrow Books, 2004. pp.27-28. The power of smiling.

11. Hurford, J. An Adaptation to the Cognitive Niche in Christiansen, M. and Kirby, S. Language Evolution, Oxford University Press, 2003. p. 46.The establishment of cooperative behaviour as a pre-adaptation for language.

12. Winston, R. Human Instinct. Bantam Books. 2002. pp.76-77. The interrelationship between the brain, meat and the digestive tract.

13. Lieberman, P. Motor Control, Speech and Evolution in Christiansen, M. and Kirby, S. Language Evolution, Oxford University Press, 2003. p 257. The ability to name objects, actions and states of being as a primitive feature of human language, present from some 5 million years ago, as surmised from the comprehension and non-speech capabilities of present-day chimpanzees.

14. Dunbar, R.I.M. Origin and Evolution of Language, in Christiansen, M. and Kirby, S. Language Evolution, Oxford University Press, 2003. p.229.The value of communal singing in relation to increasing group size and as a part of the process of developing verbal language.

15. Smith, A. The Human Body. BBC Books, 1998, p.135. The anatomy of the brain.

16. Deacon, T. The Symbolic Species. The Penguin Press, 1997. p.310. The adaptation of the brain to language.

17. Oates, J & Grayson, A. Cognitive and Language Development in Children. Blackwell Publishing Ltd, 2004. pp.76-78 The manner and context in which young children begin to understand what words mean.

18. Klein, R. The Human Career. The University of Chicago Press, 1999. pp.291-292. *Homo ergaster* adaptations to aridity.

19. Brooks, Michael. 13 Things that Don't Make Sense. ProfileBooks Ltd, 2009. pp 143 – 146. Another perspective on 'evolutionary game theory', which emphasises the importance of the individual's drive to survive, and the value of group cohesion in bringing larger numbers of young to maturity.

CHAPTER 6

1. Klein, R. The Human Career. The University of Chicago Press, 1999. p.583. Decreased dimorphism in *Homo ergaster.*

2. Finch, G. How to Study Linguistics. Palgrave Macmillan, 2003. p.24. The function of language to record.

3. Finch, G. How to Study Linguistics. Palgrave Macmillan, 2003. p.53. Alliteration and assonance. Also see www.lancaster.ac.uk (Search for Sound Symbolism.)

4. **Finch, G.** How to Study Linguistics. Palgrave Macmillan, 2003. p.41. The sense that language provides power over threatening situations.
5. **Winston, R.** Human Instinct. Bantam Books. 2002. p.72. An evolutionary explanation for morning sickness.

CHAPTER 7
1. **Pinker, S.** The Language Instinct. The Penguin Press. 1994. p.420. List of 15 families of instincts humans might possess.
2. **Klein, R.** The Human Career. The University of Chicago Press, 1999. pp.348-349. Basicranial flexion and lower siting of the larynx in *Homo ergaster.*
3. **Pinker, S.** The Language Instinct. The Penguin Press. 1994. pp.163-170. A full and detailed account of how speech sounds are produced.
4. **Lieberman, P**. Motor Control, Speech and Evolution in Christiansen, M. and Kirby, S. Language Evolution, Oxford University Press, 2003. p. 262. The vowel [i] as evidence of the selective advantage of adaptations to the vocal tract, and consequent support for the appearance of the neural capacity for speech well before *Homo sapiens.*
5. **Leakey, R.** The Origin of Humankind. Wedenfield & Nicolson. London, 1994. pp.130 - 131. More about the position of the larynx.
6. **Finch, G.** How to Study Linguistics. Palgrave Macmillan, 2003. p. 54. Communication as a cooperative process.
7. **Oates, J & Grayson, A.** Cognitive and Language Development in Children. Blackwell Publishing Ltd, 2004. p.244. Appreciation of weaknesses as an aspect of the development of a

theory of mind, and both its positive and negative consequences.

8. Diamond, J. The Rise and Fall of the Third Chimpanzee. Vintage Press, 1991. p.144. The creative role played by children in the creolization of pidgin languages. (Quoting Derek Bickerton.)

9. Whiten, A., Horner, V., de Waal, F. Letter to the journal Nature, 29.9.05. Vol.437: 737-740. Conformity to cultural norms of tool use in chimpanzees.

10. Crystal, D. Listen to Your Child. Penguin Books, 1986. pp.68-70. What young children first talk about – particular areas listed.

CHAPTER 8

1. Klein, R. The Human Career. The University of Chicago Press, 1999. pp. 582 - 583. Interpretation of fossil specimens to give a description of *Homo ergaster.*

2. Morgan, E. The Descent of the Child. Souvenir Press Ltd. 1994. p.164. The particular requirement for Omega 6 and 3 in brain tissue. Also Food and Behaviour Research website: www.fabresearch.org (Search for Dietary Sources of Omega-3 Fatty Acids, 2004.)

3. Deacon, T. The Symbolic Species. The Penguin Press, 1997. p.322. How learning and behavioural flexibility influence natural selection in the process of evolution.

4. Althaus, F. International Family Planning Perspectives, Sept. 2000. Iodine and its relevance to fertility.

5. Crowe, I. The Quest for Food. Tempus Publishing, Ltd, 2000. p.59. Why *Homo ergaster* would have been capable of migrating into territories beyond Africa.

6. Klein, R. The Human Career. The University of Chicago Press, 1999. pp.314-319. The geographic distribution of *Homo ergaster/Homo erectus*. Also Oppenheimer, S. Out of Eden. Constable & Robinson Ltd 2003. pp.14-15. *Homo ergaster* - the first human to leave Africa 1.95 million years ago.

7. Finlayson, C. The Humans who went Extinct. Oxford University Press, 2009. Pp. 14-21. The factors and processes that influenced which species survived, and their geographical distribution.

8. Klein, R. The Human Career. The University of Chicago Press, 1999. p.291, fig 5.13. Comparison between *A. afarensis* and *H. ergaster* skeletons.

9. Klein, R. Klein, R. The Human Career. The University of Chicago Press, 1999. pp. 348-349. Anatomical features relating to an ability to produce spoken language.

10. Bahn, P. Journey through the Ice Age. Weidenfeld & Nicolson, 1997. p. 209. The Aboriginal ability to commit vital habitat information to memory. Also Crowe, I. The Quest for Food. Tempus Publishing, Ltd, 2000. p.54. The necessity of having adequate spatial and sequential concepts in order to forage.

11. Klein, R. The Human Career. The University of Chicago Press, 1999. p.239. Uncertainty regarding ancestral humans' use of home bases.

12. Dunsworth, H.M. et al. Metabolic hypothesis for human altriciality. Article contributed to the Proceedings of the National Academy of Sciences of the United States of America, April 16th 2012. Five contributors present evidence suggesting that the timing of birth and the restraints on how large a baby can grow are determined by the limits of maternal metabolism – not by the dimensions of the female pelvis.

13. Leakey, R. The Origin of Humankind. Weidenfield & Nicolson. London, 1994. Ref. Spoor, F. in the journal Nature, Vol. 369, 23.6.1994. Implications of early hominin labyrinthine morphology for evolution of human bipedal locomotion.

14. Bee, H. The Developing Child. Addison-Wesley Educational Publishers, 1977. p.233 and 235. Early use of language to comment, self-direct and problem-solve.

15. Oates, J & Grayson, A. Cognitive and Language Development in Children. Blackwell Publishing Ltd, 2004. p293. The contribution of intellectual conflict within a social setting in relation to cognitive change.

16. Klein, R. The Human Career. The University of Chicago Press, 1999. pp.333-335. Descriptions of tools, sites and dates associated with the Acheulean Industrial Tradition (which began 1.7-1.6 million years ago.)

17. Bee, H. The Developing Child. Addison-Wesley Educational Publishers, 1977. p.100. Synapse formation and 'pruning' episodes in the development of the infant brain (referring to Huttenlocher, 1994.) Also Oates, J & Grayson, A. Cognitive and Language Development in Children. Blackwell Publishing Ltd, 2004. p.125. A brief summary of the process of neural growth in the brain during infancy, and how increasing specialisation leads to reduced plasticity.

CHAPTER 9

1. Ward, S. An investigation into the effectiveness of an early intervention method for delayed language development in young children. International Journal of Language and Communication Disorders, 1999, Vol 34. No 3 pp.248 - 249.   The ability to focus selectively on sound, and its fundamental importance in the development of language.

2. Oates, J & Grayson, A. Cognitive and Language Development in Children. Blackwell Publishing Ltd, 2004. p.143. The predisposition of children to develop language, the characteristic ability of the immature brain to organise itself and to serve language even without being pre-conditioned to do so.

3. Ward, S. Baby Talk. Arrow Books, 2004. p.193. The value to small children of knowing and understanding sequences of events in daily routines.

4. Deacon, T. The Symbolic Species. The Penguin Press, 1997. p.109. Children as instigators of language evolution.

5. Finch, G. How to Study Linguistics. Palgrave Macmillan, 2003. p.6. Grammar as 'organic'.

6. Ward, S. Baby Talk. Arrow Books, 2004. p.199. Understanding how the world works helps children grasp the concept of categories and this helps both in understanding the meaning of words and how language is used.

7. Finch, G. How to Study Linguistics. Palgrave Macmillan, 2003. p.87. How certain types of words occupy particular positions in connected speech.

8. Pinker, S. An Adaptation to the Cognitive Niche, in Christiansen, M. and Kirby, S. Language Evolution, Oxford University Press, 2003. p. 32. Why syntax is likely to have emerged when the events taking place in the environment were recognised as having a combinatorial quality.

9. Klein, R. The Human Career. The University of Chicago Press, 1999. p.291, Fig. 5.13 *Homo ergaster* skeleton from Nariokotome.

CHAPTER 10
1. Winston, R. Human Instinct. Bantam Books. 2002. p.321. Natural human group size as 125-150 (quoting Robin Dunbar.)
2. Pinker, S. The Language Instinct. The Penguin Press. 1994. p.306. The sequential manipulation of objects and the implications of this for the way the components of language are ordered – and how this relates to cerebral dominance.
3. Boesch, C. Transmission of Tool Use in Wild Chimpanzees. in Gibson, K, and Ingold, T. Tools, Language and Cognition in Human Evolution. Cambridge University Press, 1993. p.179. The nature of true teaching, its relative rarity (a study in Nigeria and England) and an analysis of its functions when teaching does take place.
4. Crowe, I. The Quest for Food. Tempus Publishing, Ltd, 2000. p.67. The finds at Olorgesailie.

CHAPTER 11
1. Ward, S. Baby Talk. Arrow Books, 2004. pp.218-219. The importance of using slower, louder, shorter and more tuneful speech so that the infant is aware of the sounds that make up speech. Also p.126. How intonation, pauses, slowing and stress help young infants begin to understand more of the details of connected speech.
2. Bee, H. The Developing Child. Addison-Wesley Educational Publishers, 1977. p.237. The universal habit of simplifying spoken language to babies.

3. **Ward, S.** Baby Talk. Arrow Books, 2004. pp.228-229. How small children pay attention – what they can and can't do.

4. **Klein, R.** The Human Career. The University of Chicago Press, 1999. pp.345-346 and Fig 5.47. Ref. wooden spears from Germany dated from 400,000 years ago.

5. **Crystal, D.** Listen to Your Child. Penguin Books, 1986. p.96. Children asking questions.

6. **Pinker, S.** The Language Instinct. The Penguin Press. 1994. p.40. Cultural differences in adults' attitudes to talking to small children.

7. **Klein, R.** The Human Career. The University of Chicago Press, 1999. P296. The difficulties of accurate classification of *H. heidelbergensis* remains, and of tracing what became of them.

CHAPTER 12

1. **Klein, R.** The Human Career. The University of Chicago Press, 1999. p.463.The hunting of eland at Klasies River Mouth Cave.

2. **Crowe, I.** The Quest for Food. Tempus Publishing, Ltd, 2000. pp.63-66. Also Klein, R. The Human Career. The University of Chicago Press, 1999. p.292. Fire and the consumption of meat. Also pp. 350-351. Difficulties in establishing exactly when humans first used fire.

3. **Klein, R.** The Human Career. The University of Chicago Press, 1999. p.474. The presence in early modern populations of individuals beyond reproductive age.

4. **Pinker, S.** An Adaptation to the Cognitive Niche, in Christiansen, M. and Kirby, S. Language Evolution, Oxford University Press, 2003. pp. 36-37 The FOXP2 gene being positively selected for during human evolution.

5. **Lieberman, P.** Uniquely Human. Harvard University Press, 1991. p.36. The complexities of speech perception and production.

6. **Crystal, D.** Listen to Your Child. Penguin Books, 1986. p.152. The appearance in speech of consonant 'clusters'.

7. **Pinker, S.** The Language Instinct. The Penguin Press. 1994. pp.175-181.Phonological rules in connected speech – how sounds influence their neighbours.

8. **Klein, R.** The Human Career. The University of Chicago Press, 1999. pp.505-511. The genetic evidence for modern human origins.

9. **Finch, G.** How to Study Linguistics. Palgrave Macmillan, 2003. p.32. The contribution of language to the survival process.

CHAPTER 13

1. **Ward, S.** Baby Talk. Arrow Books, 2004. pp.23-24. A baby's earliest ways of learning about the world.

2. **Ward, S.** Baby Talk. Arrow Books, 2004. p.140. A baby's intense interest in speech.

3. **Crystal, D.** Listen to Your Child. Penguin Books, 1986. pp.45-47. The emergence of melody, rhythm and tone in early infant communication.

4. **Bee, H.** The Developing Child. Addison-Wesley Educational Publishers, 1977. p.222. The naming explosion between 16 and 24 months.

5. **Finlayson, C.** The Humans who Went Extinct. Oxford University Press, 2009. p 108. The effect on species of climatic changes during the Middle Pleistocene.

6. **Crystal, D.** How Language Works. Penguin Books, 2007. p.326. Evidence of infants as young as 12 months altering the pitch of their babble –

lower in the presence of fathers, higher with mothers. Interpreted as a way of obtaining the listener's social approval.

7. Bee, H. The Developing Child. Addison-Wesley Educational Publishers, 1977. p.253. Individual temperament and personality.

8. Bee, H. The Developing Child. Addison-Wesley Educational Publishers, 1977. p.234. How children modify their speech for their listeners.

9. Oates, J & Grayson, A. Cognitive and Language Development in Children. Blackwell Publishing Ltd, 2004. p.253. The advantage to children of interacting with older siblings and a number of different adults, in developing a theory of mind.

10. Winston, R. Human Instinct. Bantam Books. 2002. pp.359-360. 'Reading' other people's minds.

11. Finch, G. How to Study Linguistics. Palgrave Macmillan, 2003. p.40. The role of language in developing a sense of identity.

12. Oppenheimer, S. Out of Eden. Constable & Robinson Ltd   2003. pp.78-80. The route and timing of the exodus from Africa by Early Modern People, the ancestors of all non-African people.

CHAPTER 14

1. Ambrose, S. Journal of Human Evolution, Vol 34, Issue 6, June 1998, pp.623-651. The global consequences of the Mt Toba eruption. Also Oppenheimer, S. Out of Eden. Constable & Robinson Ltd   2003. pp.80-82. The extent and distribution of ash from the eruption.

2. Klein, R. The Human Career. The University of Chicago Press, 1999. p.487. Neanderthals as migrants into Israel at the start of the Last Glaciation.

3. **Ward, S.** Baby Talk. Arrow Books, 2004. p.258. Children asking 'why'.

4. **Ward, S.** Baby Talk. Arrow Books, 2004. p.259. Using speech to express problems.

5. **Ward, S.** Baby Talk. Arrow Books, 2004. p.353-255. The rapid development of complex spoken language.

6. **Crystal, D.** Listen to Your Child. Penguin Books, 1986. pp.148-149. The emergence of conjunctions.

7. **Bee, H.** The Developing Child. Addison-Wesley Educational Publishers, 1977. p.227. The 'grammar explosion', 27-36 months.

8. **Aitchison, J.** The Seeds of Speech. Cambridge University Press, 2000. p.130. (Ref Bickerton, D. A 'bioprogram' view of early language.) Also Bee, H. The Developing Child. Addison-Wesley Educational Publishers, 1977. p.228. The creation of novel sentences.

9. **Finch, G.** How to Study Linguistics. Palgrave Macmillan, 2003. p 85. The rules governing the underlying sound structures and meanings of a language. Also pp.98-99. The creation of phrases and sentences.

10. **Oates, J & Grayson, A.** Cognitive and Language Development in Children. Blackwell Publishing Ltd, 2004. p. 117. Discussion of contrasting views on the degree to which children's neural development is innately determined, epigenetics emphasising the role of interactions with the outside environment.

11. **BBC Science and Nature** website: www.bbc.co.uk/sn/tvradio/programmes/horizon/ghostgenes.shtml The Ghost in your Genes. How events affecting grandparents appear to impinge on their grandchildren.

CHAPTER 15
1. Klein, R. The Human Career. The University of Chicago Press, 1999. pp.498-499. A description of modern humans in comparison to other hominids.
2. Klein, R. The Human Career. The University of Chicago Press, 1999. p.589, Table 8.1. Some Attributes of Fully Modern Human Behaviour Detectable in the Archaeological Record Beginning 50-40 thousand Years Ago.
3. Oppenheimer, S. Out of Eden. Constable & Robinson Ltd 2003. pp.110-113. An alternative view to that of Klein, above, of the genetic heritage of Fully Modern Humans, giving a date of origin around 190,000 years ago. He argues that the genetic basis for modern human behaviours including speech must have been present in the ancestral humans who left Africa about 80,000 years ago.
4. Finch, G. How to Study Linguistics. Palgrave Macmillan, 2003. p.41and 52. Playing with language, and the mixing of senses in relation to food and speech.
5. Finch, G. How to Study Linguistics. Palgrave Macmillan, 2003. p.176. The processes whereby new words arise in a language.
6. Finch, G. How to Study Linguistics. Palgrave Macmillan, 2003. p.162, 163. Comments on the fact that language is never totally adequate for what we desire to express, and what strategies language adopts to deal with this burden.
7. Aitchison, J. The Seeds of Speech. Cambridge University Press, 2000. p.25. What language is good at doing.
8. Crystal, D. How Language Works. Penguin Books, 2007. p.361. How languages converge as a

consequence of people coming into contact with each other.

9. Pinker, S. The Language Instinct. The Penguin Press. 1994. pp.170-172. The range of human speech sounds across all languages.

10. Ward, S. Baby Talk. Arrow Books, 2004. p.52. How an infant's repertoire of sounds becomes that of his own language.

11. Finch, G. How to Study Linguistics. Palgrave Macmillan, 2003. pp.128-140. How words acquire meaning, and the different levels of meaning in any act of communication.

12. Finch, G. How to Study Linguistics. Palgrave Macmillan, 2003. p.22. One of the 'micro functions' of spoken language – to release energy.

13. Metro News, www.metro.co.uk (Search for Mumsnet teenage slang). Slang translations according to Mumsnet users, June 2013: yolo – you only live once, blemboss – person smoking just to show off, peng – rather good, bounce – to leave, hench – strong and muscular.

14. Klein, R. The Human Career. The University of Chicago Press, 1999. pp.514-517. Discussions concerning biological and cultural change.

15. Finch, G. How to Study Linguistics. Palgrave Macmillan, 2003. p.149. Metaphor as a creative device in language.

16. Crystal, D. How Language Works.Penguin Books, 2007. p88. The age at which children recognise some meanings if conveyed solely by intonation.

17. Sykes, B. The Seven Daughters of Eve. Bantam Press, 2001. The genetic origins of modern humans.

18. Klein, R. The Human Career. The University of Chicago Press, 1999. p.513.

Enkapune Ya Muto Cave and the eggshell beads.

EPILOGUE
1. Zawawi, S. A Swahili book of Names. Africa World Press, 1993. p.22. Interpreting the meaning of the name 'Africa'.
2. Rudgely, R. Lost Civilizations of the Stone Age. Century, 1998. pp.36-45. The controversial American linguist Joseph Greenberg's 17 language families, and examples of Bengston and Ruhlen's 45 global etymologies.
3. Feral Children on **YouTube.**

BIBLIOGRAPHY

Aitchison, J. The Seeds of Speech. Cambridge University Press, 2000.

Althaus, F. International Family Planning Perspectives. Sept. 2000.

Ambrose, S. Journal of Human Evolution, Vol 34, Issue 6, June 1998.

Atkinson, Q. Report in the journal Science, 15/4/11.

Bahn, P. Journey through the Ice Age. Weidenfeld & Nicolson, 1997.

Bee, H. The Developing Child. Addison-Wesley Educational Publishers, 1977.

Boesch, C. Transmission of Tool Use in Wild Chimpanzees in Tools, Language and Cognition in Human Evolution. (Eds.) Gibson, K, and Ingold, T. Cambridge University Press, 1993.

Brooks, M.13 Things that Don't Make Sense. ProfileBooks Ltd, 2009.

Christiansen, M. and Kirby, S. Language Evolution. Oxford University Press, 2005.

Cooke, J. and Williams, D. Working with Children's Language. Winslow Press, 1991.

Crowe, I. The Quest for Food. Tempus Publishing Ltd, 2000.

Crystal, D. Listen to Your Child. Penguin Books, 1986. How Language Works. Penguin Books, 2007

Deacon, T. The Symbolic Species. The Penguin Press, 1997.

Diamond, J. The Rise and Fall of the Third Chimpanzee. Vintage Press, 1991.

Downer, J. Supersense. BBC Books, 1988.

Dunbar, R. Origin and Evolution of Language, in Christiansen, M. and Kirby, S. Language Evolution, Oxford University Press, 2003.

Dunsworth, H.M. et al. Metabolic hypothesis for human altriciality. Article contributed to the Proceedings of the National Academy of Sciences of the United States of America, April 16th 2012.

Finch, G. How to Study Linguistics. Palgrave Macmillan, 2003.

Finlayson, C. The Humans who went Extinct. Oxford University Press, 2009.

Gibson, K. (Ed.) Tools, Language and Cognition in Human Evolution. Cambridge University Press, 1993.

Goldin-Meadow, S. When does Gesture become Language? in Gibson, K, and Ingold, T. (Eds) Tools, Language and Cognition in Human Evolution. Cambridge University Press, 1993.

Goodall, J. The Chimpanzees of Gombe. The Belknap Press of Harvard University, 1986.

Hurford, J. The Language Mosaic in Christiansen, M. and Kirby, S. Language Evolution, Oxford University Press, 2003.

Klein, R. The Human Career. The University of Chicago Press, 1999.

Leakey, R. The Origin of Humankind. Weidenfield & Nicolson. 1994.

Lieberman, P. Uniquely Human. Harvard University Press, 1991. Also: Motor Control, Speech and Evolution, in Christiansen, M. and Kirby, S. Language Evolution, Oxford University Press, 2003.

Merenstein, G. & Gardner, S. Handbook of Neonatal Intensive Care. Mosby, 1993.

Morgan, E. The Descent of the Child. Souvenir Press Ltd. 1994.

Morrison, D. Pothier, P. & Horr, K. Sensory-Motor Dysfunction and Therapy in Infancy and Early Childhood. Charles C. Thomas, 1978.

Oates, J & Grayson, A. Cognitive and Language Development in Children. Blackwell Publishing Ltd, 2004.

Oppenheimer, S. Out of Eden. Constable & Robinson Ltd 2003.

Pinker, S. The Language Instinct. The Penguin Press. 1994. Also: An Adaptation to the Cognitive Niche, in Christiansen, M. and Kirby, S. Language Evolution, Oxford University Press, 2003.

Rudgely, R. Lost Civilizations of the Stone Age. Century, 1998.

Smith, A. The Human Body. BBC books, 1998.

Snowdon, C.   A Comparative Approach to Language Parallels in Tools, Language and Cognition in Human Evolution. (Eds.) Gibson, K, and Ingold, T. Cambridge University Press, 1993.

Stoppard, M. Complete Baby and Child Care. Dorling Kindersley, 1995.

Studdert-Kennedy, M. and Goldstein, L. The Gestural Origin of Discrete Infinity, in Christiansen, M. and Kirby, S. Language Evolution, Oxford University Press, 2003.

Sykes, B. The Seven Daughters of Eve. Bantam Press, 2001.

Ward, S. Baby Talk. Arrow Books, 2004. Also International Journal of Language and Communication Disorders, 1999, Vol 34. An investigation into the effectiveness of an early intervention method for delayed language development in young children.

Whiten, A., Horner, V., de Waal, F. Letter to the journal Nature, 29.9.05. Vol.437: Conformity to cultural norms of tool use in chimpanzees.

Winston, R. Human Instinct. Bantam Books. 2002.

Zawawi, S. A Swahili Book of Names. Africa World Press, 1993.

WEBSITES.
Laetoli Footprints:
www.humanorigins.si.edu/evidence/behavior/laeto
li-footprint-trails.
Aquatic Ape theory:
www.theguardian.com/science/2013/apr/27/aquati
c-ape-theory-primate-evolution .
Sound symbolism: www.lancaster.ac.uk (Search
for Sound Symbolism.)
Omega-3: Food and Behaviour Research website:
www.fabresearch.org
Epigenetics:
www.bbc.co.uk/sn/tvradio/programmes/horizon/gh
ostgenes.shtml
Slang translations according to Mumsnet users
Metro News: www.metro.co.uk
Feral Children: YouTube.